# Perennial Philosophy

# Praise for *Perennial Philosophy*

In this lucid explanation of perennial philosophy, Arthur Versluis reveals this tradition—so often described as esoteric and inaccessible—to be closer to our interests and experience than many of us have realized. Versluis has distilled an immense amount of scholarship into this small volume, but its brevity is deceiving. Like the culmination to any alchemical work, *Perennial Philosophy* is a powerful tincture that—once imbibed—transports receptive readers to a world in which they are part of a spiritual hierarchy that links heaven to earth. Arthur Versluis has distilled an immense amount of scholarship to produce a disarmingly accessible, lucid, and deeply penetrating study of the great philosophic traditions that underlie Western culture. Versluis concisely explains what perennial philosophy is and what it isn't. The clarity of his prose makes this deep book a pleasure to read. A remarkable achievement!

—Gregory Shaw, author of *Theurgy and the Soul: The Neoplatonism of Iamblichus*

This brilliant little book, written with stunning clarity, offers an entirely new perspective on what "perennial philosophy" actually means and entails. This is a return to the real philosophical quest, almost entirely forgotten by the academic world: a going beyond the limited self, to experience our kinship with the greater world and the deepest levels of reality, which results in a transformation of the self and a realization of our human nature.

For anyone interested in the roots of our philosophical tradition, or what a living philosophy could look like today and in the future—a philosophy that actually inspires and fertilizes culture, art, and human experience—this book is indispensable.

—David Fideler, author of *Restoring the Soul of the World* and other books and essays.

This book is about transcendence: self-transcendence. It traces a pathway to such self-transcendence from Plato (Pythagoras and the Orphic mysteries), through Plotinus, Damascius, Meister Eckhart and Emerson. Perennial Philosophy unveils a contemplative way often referred to as " mysticism" that leads to a selfless, compassionate caring for all existence, from the animate to the inanimate, since all that exists expresses divine creation. The book has no footnotes and yet is scholarly. It records a perennial way of being-in-the-world that contrasts sharply with the way most of us live and see, and is about a past that offers glimpses of a better future. To read it is to question the contemporary understanding of who we are, and what we are capable of becoming. It is medicine for difficult times.

—Robert E. Carter, Trent University, author of *Encounter with Enlightenment*, *The Kyoto School*, and many other books.

This short work is one of the most important books I have read in many years. It is also one of the bravest. The author sets out to reclaim and revivify the philosophia perennis for an era in which it is officially shunned, buried in fashionable relativisms or else usurped by obscurantists. Written in an even, steady tone without academic pretensions and with unfailing clarity, it reaffirms the enduring tenets of Platonism and sets out the case for it as a universal and timeless heritage in which a transcendent vision is paramount. The author carefully places this against the entire range of those contemporary prejudices that lock us into limited and limiting intellectual perspectives. It is a work of hope. It is a work that dares to proclaim a commitment to truth. It is a work that points the way out of the gloom of the cave. More than any other recent book it offers us a fresh start and a chance to rediscover, as T.S. Eliot described it, "what is lost and found and lost again and again."

—Rod Blackhirst, LaTrobe University, author of *Primordial Alchemy and Modern Religion.*

This book is colloquial and conversational. It presents an overview of Platonism from the master himself to Emerson in the context of contemporary debates. The author is a devoted Platonist, and his presentation of their doctrines is perfectly orthodox, above all in the absolute priority he gives to intellectual vision, the Vision of the Good. This emphasis alone is a huge achievement. The book is remarkable also for its generosity of tone. To the enlightened eye, no doubt, everything is full of Being. But it is difficult to maintain at all times that warm dispassion which takes the whole world under its wing. The author achieves this simply through the quality of his discriminations. So sharp and apt are the distinctions he makes between competing contemporary doctrines the book is continually illuminating and never tendentious. This reader was forever saying "Ah!"

—Roger Sworder, LaTrobe University, author of *Mathematical Plato,* and *Science and Religion in Archaic Greece* as well as *A Contrary History of the West.*

# Perennial Philosophy

# Arthur Versluis

Library of Congress Cataloging-in-Publication Data

Versluis, Arthur, 1959-
  Perennial philosophy / Arthur Versluis.
    pages cm
  ISBN 978-1-59650-016-7 (alk. paper)
  1. Religion--Philosophy. 2. Philosophy and religion. 3. Transcendence (Philosophy) 4. Self--Religious aspects. 5. Mysticism. I. Title.
  BL51.V475 2015
  149'.3--dc23
                          2015029412

Text set in Caslon

EPub ISBN: 978-159650-017-4

The paper used in this publication meets the minimum
requirements of ANSI/NISO Z39.48-1992 (R 1997) (Permanence of
Paper).

Cover image from Tintagel courtesy of the author
New Cultures Press
Minneapolis, Minnesota

Visit us at
www.newcultures.org
Printed and bound in the United States of America.

18 17 16 15      1 2 3 4 5 6 7 8 9 10              1st

# Contents

# Introduction

This is a book about perennial philosophy, or *philosophia perennis*. Much of what is in this book always has challenged prevailing ideologies—as the death of Socrates symbolizes. Socrates, the wisest man in Athens, "corrupted youths" and so was sentenced to death. And perennial philosophy still challenges prevailing orthodoxies today, just as it no doubt will in the future. But that perennial philosophy is not in fashion at this or that time is not a convincing argument against it. This book presents perennial philosophy not as syncretic, or combining different faiths, but as the natural consequence of a particular kind of inward knowledge that, although it can come spontaneously, is generally the result of inward discipline and spiritual practice. In other words, this small book is both an introduction to and a handbook for perennial philosophy, which ultimately is experiential.

Perennial philosophy often has been presented in confusing ways, chiefly by attempting to make it a result of combining different religious traditions, or by claiming that there is a single religion behind or inside the different world religious traditions. But the approach of the *philosophia perennis* is neither of these, and although the second (the concept of a single religion behind or inside different religions) may or may not be warranted, it is simply not intrinsic to perennial philosophy, which is not a method for comparing religions anyway.

Thomas Merton wrote in his *Asian Journal* that "We are already one. But we imagine that we are not. So what we have to recover is our original unity. What we have to be is what we are." Such a perspective goes completely against the current academic fashion, in which "God is not one," as a recent book title has it. But perennial philosophy does not mean that all religions are one. Rather, it means that there is an underlying basic shared human metaphysical reality, and that is what Merton is referring to, an insight that resulted from his traveling Eastward, both literally and figuratively. Platonism and Hermetism are the model for perennial philosophy in the European tradition, and Vedanta serves an analogous role in India. Buddhism is distinctive from all of these, of course, not least because of its unique emphasis on emptiness. And perennial philosophy does not hold that all these traditions are identical, nor that they all point toward exactly the same goals or kinds of realization.

What is perennial in perennial philosophy is truth. The heart of perennial philosophy is what is suggested also by neuroscientific research— that there are human responses characteristic of particular training and experiences, and that those can be charted cartographically. If one discovers what is true, then it is true not only for oneself, but also for others. Perennial philosophy does not claim that all religious or spiritual traditions are the same, but rather that the human search for and realization of truth is perennial, that is, it can be experienced by different people in diverse circumstances. Again, what is perennial in perennial philosophy is truth, or to put it another way, what is perennial is experience of the ground of being, which, if it is true, is true and verifiable by others.

Perennial philosophy points to individual spiritual experience; and Platonism, Hermetism, Vedanta, and Buddhism all are based on direct individual realizations, on the experiential transformation and illumination of the individual. That is what Aldous Huxley's book, *The Perennial Philosophy,* centered on, and that was how he defined perennial philosophy. The word "perennial" in this context means that human beings can go through transformative and illuminative processes that are intrinsically open to us as human beings; that people have gone through, are going through, or may go through such a process in the past, present, and future (hence it perennially recurs). The word "philosophy" does not have the meaning of "an abstract theoretical system constructed by discursive reason," but rather that of "a virtuous life leading to the realization of love (philo) and wisdom (sophia)."

Now you might ask why we need another book on perennial philosophy. Huxley's book, first published in 1945, presents a series of thematically linked quotations from a wide array of sources both Asian and European, with a focus on mystics and mystical transformation and awakening. *The Perennial Philosophy* had a long and influential subsequent history, and is visible behind much of the California counterculture of the 1960s and 1970s, as well as behind New Age and related movements of the late twentieth and early twenty-first centuries. Of course, there is another modern intellectual current known as "Traditionalism," which is also often regarded as a form of perennialism too. But what we are describing here is at once both ancient and new, and in some respects distinct from these recent variants.

In truth, the concept of perennial philosophy absolutely needs clarification in the wake of so many developments, new interpretations, and changes in cultural-social contexts. The terms "perennialism" and "perennial philosophy" have lost any crispness of meaning. This is in part because these terms are often defined by opponents, who express great alarm at any hint of what they term "essentialism"—a term that as we will see, is not so effective an accusation as it is often assumed to be. Nonetheless, many academics, particularly in the humanities, rejected out of hand all "metanarratives" and normative "truth claims," asserting instead in abstruse and opaque language what amounts finally to a kind of rarified nihilism. Given the waning of these intellectual movements and developments, perennial philosophy certainly calls for new consideration.

As we describe it here, perennial philosophy at heart is Platonism. Platonism, in this context, is philosophy not as a product of combative discursive reasoning, but as a way of life. It is existential, in the sense that it is centered in encouraging one to live a virtuous life, but also because it proposes a metaphysics centered on the individual's potential realization of self-other transcendence. Hence what is "perennial" about perennial philosophy is its call to the individual to live a better life and, potentially at least, to "return to the One," that is, to contemplatively realize inner unity.

Now Platonism is sometimes imported into monotheism, so that one then finds Christian Platonism (the ur-figure for which is of course Dionysius the Areopagite), Islamic Platonism (which in effect becomes Sufism) and Jewish Platonism (to some extent, perhaps, in Kabbalah). But for all that, Platonism is prior to and distinct from the various monotheisms, and it provides a Western tradition that is closest to Buddhist and Vedantic religious philosophies.

Hence perennial philosophy is inherently esoteric, in that those who practice it are engaged in a contemplative ascent that cannot be fully understood only through discursive descriptions of it. Discursive descriptions as read by an outsider and non-participant are exoteric, and as such give only indirect access to the actual contemplative experiences that accompany the individual's inward realization of Platonic metaphysics. Platonism in this regard is a philosophical translation for individuals of what previously had belonged to the Greek Mysteries as group revelations of transcendence (about which participants were famously and for the most part effectively sworn to secrecy), and in both cases the center of the tradition is experiential and transmutational.

In this respect perennial philosophy is fundamentally different than contemporary academia in general and academic philosophy in particular, where discursive reason alone is hegemonic. The dominance of discursive reason as a mode of consciousness, so prevalent in contemporary intellectual life, has many consequences, not the least of which is that other modes of consciousness are studiously ignored. Contemporary academic philosophy, by so emphasizing discursive reason, reinforces prevailing social tendencies toward dualism and materialism, separates individual subjects from objects of study, and appears to remove even the possibility of philosophy as a way of life. Contemporary academia—in its zeal to insist on a posture of objectivity based on an imagined hegemony of discursive reason, and in its prevailing fear of such bugaboos as "essentialism" and "metanarratives"—in effect stands for nothing. It is for the most part as if contemporary academics are adrift in an ocean without map, compass, sextant, or any other means of navigation—and insist that no means of navigation is acceptable!

Perennial philosophy, on the other hand, presents us with a map, a compass, a sextant—it offers us ways to navigate. Since it is so central to the history of Western European culture and religion, it is incumbent on us at least to become familiar with it. But it also may provide us with more than antiquarian knowledge. For the purpose of perennial philosophy is, ultimately, teleological and soteriological: it points us toward the higher meanings and purposes of human life. It has much to offer us concerning the nature of our world and of ourselves, in particular our relationship to nature, and the nature of our own consciousness. It offers us a coherent larger metaphysical context and significance to our lives.

What is more, as perennial, it belongs as much to our present and future as it does to our past. In what follows, I present perennial philosophy in an existential context, and what is more, recognize that it now exists in an intellectual world no longer restricted to one religious or cultural ambience, but inhabited by many religions. Among these, the advent of Asian religions in the West has been especially influential, and we cannot discuss perennial philosophy (which came into being in the Greco-Roman world) in a contemporary context without recognizing signal points where it intersects with Hinduism and Buddhism.

The fundamental insight of perennial philosophy is that truth is unitary and it can be perceived by human cognition. Plato describes this kind of cognition as akin to a spark, which can be transmitted from a teacher to a pupil. The spark is of the same nature as a fire, and it is also light, illumination—but as perceived by human cognition. Perennial philosophy is insight into what is perennial, what is always accessible to us because it is the very nature of cognition itself—it is self-reflective and self-transcendent awareness.

What follows are essays in the classical sense, forays outside the city into the pastoral landscape and into wilderness, into the mountains and valleys, perhaps even across great bodies of water, in the tradition represented by Pythagoras and Plato, Plotinus, and Damascius. These four figures mark the full gamut of the Pythagorean-Platonic tradition in antiquity, and with these four figures we will journey, on our way marking the stars and planets, orienting ourselves with our intellectual compass and sextant on the earth and in the universe. The sextant, compass, and map together are perennial philosophy, and with its assistance, we can find our way and, what is more, understand our path's meaning.

Perennial philosophy, as we explore it here, is esoteric in the purest sense of the word—which, after all, has its origins in the initiatory tradition of Pythagoreanism, and no doubt before that and after, in the mystery traditions whose origins are no longer visible to us. Perennial philosophy is actually secret in our present age, because nearly all the prejudices we inherit from our time are opposed to it and to the insights it offers. And yet it is an open secret, because it is transmitted in texts, and the key texts are all available to us now. We are in a unique moment in history, perhaps the end of an age, it is true, but also at that unique point when what always has been there is visible to us now in an unexpected way.

That is what this book is about: it is a book about the open secret of perennial philosophy. It is not meant for those who think the only things that exist are those that can be grasped with the hands. It is not meant for those who long for some historical revolution that they imagine is right around the corner, and in whose wake blood no doubt would flow, as it did so copiously in the tragic political religions of the twentieth century. This book is not meant for true believers. It is meant for those who know that there is more to who we are and to where we are than what we find in the prevailing ideologies of the day, both inside and outside the academy. If you have read this far, perhaps it is meant for you.

# Chapter One

# Leaving the Cave

Already, you may have begun to surmise that this is an unusual book, and perhaps you have the odd feeling that in reading it, you're remembering something that you've forgotten, but sensed was there. That is in fact how things really are. Central to perennial philosophy is *anamnesis,* which is a very strange linguistic construction that means, literally, *not-forgetting. Not-amnesia.* Isn't that a peculiar way to express it? A kind of double negative, a *not not,* as it were. But that very double negative, *anamnesis,* expresses the heart of perennial philosophy, because we find ourselves, in our ordinary consciousness in this world, to be living as if we were in a cave. And perennial philosophy consists in instructions on how to *leave the cave.*

What is the cave in which we dwell? It has some distinguishing characteristics. It is material—densely material. In it, it is hard to even imagine that there is a world outside the cave, and that what we see in it are moving shadows and flickering images, like a *movie,* as the antiquated term has it. We are caught up in a narrative in front of us, and we believe or at least react as if what we see is real and even all that exists. Hence it is also emotional, because we react to what we see—we become caught up in the narrative that is presented to us by society. And we even believe that what we see is the culmination of human history, and that everything has led up to the narrative we now are observing in the dim light of our cave.

This is the metaphor that Plato gave us in *The Republic:* we are like prisoners in a cave, seeing shadows cast by moving figures, and never realizing that there is an *outside* to the cave, that above and outside there is a real sun, a real earth, that outside the cave is *reality.* But in our present state of consciousness, we cannot even look for what is outside, because we take our cavern for real, for the only reality, dark and constrained though it is. Of course, it is possible that there is a bit of a trick to understanding this, because to think that this cave-world is to be understood as completely *other* than what is outside it, well, that would be a mistake.

And what is perennial philosophy, in the context of this cave-metaphor? Perennial philosophy is the result of someone who has gotten outside the cave and seen the real world. Our ordinary discursive consciousness, from this perspective, is a kind of sleep or forgetting, symbolized also by the river Lethe whose waters induce forgetfulness. But we can awaken from this condition, which also is described in the ancient Mysteries as a kind of death. The Mysteries were said to bring life, illumination, awakening, and that is what is conveyed also in the term *anamnesis.* Perennial philosophy is a kind of *waking up*.

Waking up to what? To knowledge, to awareness, to the light. If ordinary life can be likened to a cave, then to awaken is to go outside the cave from the darkness into the light of the sun. The sun, here, is consciousness. And according to perennial philosophy, illumination includes but also transcends our ordinary discursive consciousness. In the cave, we are divided; we appear to be separated selves opposed to one another, competitive, reactive, emotional, fearful. Outside the cave, in this metaphor, our ordinary discursive consciousness is illuminated by a light whose very nature is consciousness pervading us all (humans and nature both). This new kind of illuminated consciousness is nascent when we are in the cave; it is born when we are outside the cave and in the light.

And of course Plato's metaphor continues, because when someone has gotten outside the cave into the light, naturally, after becoming oriented there, eventually he wants to return in order to rescue the others who are still trapped in the darkness. That is only a natural impulse, isn't it? But—and here is a real insight offered by Plato—when he returns to the cave, the inhabitants do not welcome him, but rather disbelieve his assertions of an "outside," of freedom and illumination. They do not want to leave; they do not want to hear about liberation, and perhaps they even turn on him. What Plato conveyed, in the last part of his parable, is a profound insight about Western culture, and perhaps about humanity as a whole: it is possible that many of us, perhaps most of us, don't want to be saved. We fear our own liberation, and turn on those who offer it to us, because we cannot really understand what they are offering.

And yet our natural home is not the cave. Foundational to Platonism is the insight that the light, the sun of knowledge, the warmth and pleasure of shared illumination, this is our natural inheritance, our original condition, which (having drunk the waters of Lethe) we have forgotten. To be illuminated is to *not-forget*. With this parable, Plato introduces us to the essential opening through which we must pass to enter into perennial philosophy. This doorway opens into the recognition, the *re-cognition* that there is truth, and that we can perceive it for ourselves. Most contemporary narratives deny the very concept of truth; they claim, instead, like the Sophists, that there is no truth, only the hegemony of discursive reason and the illusion of a reactive self. Only the cave, only darkness, and forgetting.

But it is not so. Yet this is what nearly everyone wants to tell you. What passes for religion is as likely to do so as what passes for science. An assumed cynicism pervades their claims; they pretend to be sure, but they know, on some level, that they are not at all certain, that they are in a fundamental way, the most fundamental way of all, *insecure*. One might even think that sophisticated theoretical or theological or doctrinal systems were a kind of compensation for this basic insecurity, as if, were the system built sturdily enough, it might make up for that nagging absence at the foundation. Some even want to extirpate anything that looks like perennial philosophy, as if by doing so, they could somehow restore their own foundation. But in that way, of course, restoration is impossible.

In perennial philosophy, there is only one way of restoration or awakening, and that is ascent to a vision of truth. In the fifth book of his *Republic,* Plato has Socrates remark that the true philosophers are those who are lovers of the vision of truth. There are those who can see only beautiful earthly things, but in so doing, they live as in a dream, whereas the mind of one who rises to a vision of absolute beauty is awakened. The former is caught in opinion, that is, in emotional reactivity, whereas the latter has knowledge, that is, direct knowledge of the nature of being itself. Ignorance corresponds to not-being, or with the facsimile of being (cave-dwelling), whereas knowledge is of being itself. Being, here, is absolute and timeless; and it is also both truth and beauty, or true and beautiful. To ascend to a vision of these is to attain wisdom; it is to be a sage.

One who has left the cave and dwells in the light of the sun is a sage with relation to those who remain below, and to produce a sage is, after all, the goal of perennial philosophy. If you are reading about this, perhaps it stirs memories for you. Plato, of course, also employs the word "philosopher," meaning "lover of wisdom," which he also likens to a kind of mantic madness. Much as a lover becomes intoxicated with and even mad for his beloved, so the sage becomes intoxicated with the incomparable beauty and illumination of what is beyond or above the sensory realm. The philosopher ascends as if on wings to see, not just knowledge as usually understood, but knowledge of the absolute, or of the absolute existent, truth and beauty inexpressible and beyond conception, without color, without form, intangible, and yet pervading one with the joy of perceiving it.

In *Phaedrus,* Plato shifts his metaphor to an ascent on wings into the empyrean, and here he openly uses the language of initiation into the ancient Mysteries. The initiate ascends by the lightness of wings to imbibe divine beauty, wisdom, and goodness above, though it is also possible to sink down, weighted by one's attachments and aversions to the earthly realm. But the sage ascends into the mysteries of the perfect, which in turn perfects him, for we become what we gaze upon. The philosopher ascends with wings to gaze upon divine beauty that is truth, which is also a recollection or remembering of what always has been. This vision of the perfect is really a return to our native realm.

Perhaps in reading such a description, something answers to it in you. Perhaps you recall, even just a bit, the light and love and life of true being, which is in truth beyond being (*meontic*). To us belongs a celestial memory, a beatific vision of living light and beauty, simple and calm and happy, and yet it is not only a memory in the usual sense, for it is also an indication of what we can know once again, or remember, *anamnesis,* not-forgetting. This is what initiation into philosophical mystery means, not discursive reason alone, nattering back and forth, but visionary ascent and awareness that is both to see and to become at once. It is illumination.

And such mysteries cannot be conveyed in writing, but only alluded to, because they have to be experienced. In fact, the written word can be deceptive; it can seem to take the place of what it only indicates, and what is more, it can be misunderstood.

It is not difficult for one to misinterpret a work—indeed, much of Plato's dialogues and letters today are presented, often, as entirely other than they actually are, if attention is paid to them at all. Plato is accused of being a dualist, a proto-totalitarian, and all sorts of other things, as though his works were not really about precisely what he alludes to throughout them—for they are about the mysteries; they are meant to initiate us into spiritual life.

The ancients were acutely aware of the problem of writing, and this is why the ancient mysteries were never written discursively, not the mysteries of the Egyptians and Greeks, and not the mysteries of the Druids. Of the ancient Mysteries, almost nothing was committed to writing, and of the Druidic College, nothing either; these were strictly initiatic—spoken or whispered teachings. Even Plato's works are largely dialogues between multiple characters, and often include parables, metaphors, and allusion. Allusive and elusive, Plato himself, whose work is the headwaters of perennial philosophy, is midway between the ancient oral traditions and writing.

From Plato on, and especially with the advent of Christianity, initiation was largely conveyed elliptically, through writing and images. Perennial philosophy rarely has had continuity over even several generations; it was, rather, something to be discovered anew. And that is still how it is today. It is not different now than it was a thousand or two thousand years ago. Indeed, it may be that only to a few is the possibility granted to leave the cave; that only now and then is there someone who is haunted by memories of light and life and joy that does not quite seem to belong to this sensory world, but that we glimpse through it, often in wild nature's intimations of immortality, in the luminous bodies of the sky, as in a great assembly hall whose pillars are of light.

Ours is an age of enforced egalitarianism, as though if one man runs faster than another, the logical solution would be to cripple the faster of them. But that is not how nature is—nature gifts some and leaves others without. There is such a thing as a spiritual aristocracy, whether we like it or not, perennial philosophy tells us. Some belong to the species *homo religiosus,* and are naturally inclined to remember, to seek illumination, and to live the solitary, eremitic life. Now and then, we encounter one another, sometimes only via the written word, but that is an encounter, too, often more living than any other, because it is a meeting of minds irrespective of time or distance.

And so it may have to be for us, too. Perhaps these few written indications will have to do. Or perhaps you will find your way to someone able to guide you. Either way, though, there are keys hidden in nature herself, and it is always possible to rediscover them. Perennial philosophy is perennial not only in human culture, but also in the patterns of nature. It is not as though leaving the cave means ignoring or abandoning this earth and all its mysteries. Rather, it means waking up to what is here. And that awakening includes the treasures hidden in nature; it is a kind of universal key. What that key opens, we turn to next.

# Chapter Two

# Nature's Secrets

As above, so below, the well-known Hermetic aphorism has it, but it might be better expressed: as inwardly, so outwardly. According to perennial philosophy, we have the capacity for understanding both nature and ourselves in very different ways than can be expressed in the objectifying terms of discursive reason. There is between us and nature a hidden series of connections that we intuit, sometimes, but that remain most of the time literally *occult*, that is, obscured, hidden from our ordinary sight. And so it is for most of us most of the time. But every now and then, we glimpse something in the wild that reminds us of the hidden patterns of our world, and that calls us homeward. After all, coming to understand perennial philosophy is coming to understand nature's language.

Through technology, we have gained a particular kind of power over the natural world, which we can objectify and manipulate, but in so doing, we do not realize that other ways of understanding the world become occluded and lost to us. We are lured by the flow of images and shallow words from our technological tethers and we do not see where we are, or what is within us. Immersed in our busy world of machines, noise, chatter, and constant activity, we find ourselves ever further from what once connected us to the cosmos around us, but now seems nearly gone. Perennial philosophy reminds us of the other dimensions of the cosmos, the hidden patterns of nature. But if we cannot recognize or heed it, then it is as if it does not exist for us at all.

That there are patterns in the cosmos, scientists know. But the ultimate *meaning* of those patterns, that, scientists cannot give us. Ultimate meaning requires religious philosophy. And perennial philosophy, which begins with awakening, with *anamnesis,* or not-forgetting, sheds light not only on ultimate things, but also on the nature of the cosmos that reflects those ultimate things. According to perennial philosophy, the world that we see, the stars, the sun, moon, and planets, the waters of the sea, and the mountains, the wind and the clouds, the flowers and trees, the fish and the birds and the animals, all that belongs to our natural world manifests numbers and patterns that are beyond them.

From the perspective of perennial philosophy, time is not separate from but manifests timelessness. The unfolding of patterns in nature has its origin in timeless numbers and geometry that, in turn, are principles radiating from the timeless realm of order prior to the cosmos that we see now. What we see now seems limited to a particular point in linear time and to particular coordinates in three-dimensional space, and seems only that, but perennial philosophy reminds us of what is behind and above that which we see. The Pythagorean, the Platonic, and the Druidic traditions have at their center metaphysics, but in their application are cosmological.

At the heart of nature's secrets is the emergence of two from one, symbolized in this way:

*

\*    \*

Here, the one divides into two, which brings about the primordial form of the triad. When we look at the ancient stone monuments of Britain and Western Europe, we see the triangle repeated in the geometry of the sacred sites. And one can also see the threefold pattern in the circles or spheres that can be inscribed within the sacred geometry of many collections of standing stones. The pattern of three can be understood both as triangles and as overlapping spheres.

Three overlapping spheres can be understood as symbolizing the domains of cosmological manifestation from above to below, from heaven to earth. Above is the circle of heaven, intersecting with the realm of human culture, in turn intersecting with the realm of nature. Each overlap forms a *vesica piscis,* that is, a form resembling a fish or an eye, and the human domain includes both the heavenly and the earthly *vesica piscis.* Seen in this way, human culture includes physical dwellings, tools and instruments (earth); songs, poems, and stories that explain their meaning; and the religious philosophy (heaven) that informs them. Julius Caesar remarked that the Gauls were divided into husbandmen, warriors, and priests (Druids). Diodoros Siculus observed in passing, and Strabo developed the observation that in addition to the druids (responsible for religious lore, philosophy, and ritual) the ancient far Western European culture included also bards (the singers and poets) and ovates, whose purview was the natural world. These three groups also correspond to the three hierarchic and interconnected spheres of human culture.

Of these three groups, the first, those responsible for religious philosophy and ritual, were reputed by the ancients to have special knowledge of the patterns of the stars and planets, sun and moon, and also to have considerable mathematical knowledge. And indeed, throughout far Western Europe, there are megaliths of great weight and size, set in semi-circular or other patterns, and they reveal in their arrangements ancient knowledge of astronomical, geometrical, and mathematical relationships. This knowledge was said by some Roman authors to be linked to an ancient mythical land of the far north, called Hyperborea.

Hyperborea is a mystery—it is said by some to be a mythical name for the land of the Celts, but locating it on a map seems a doubtful proposition, for it seems closer to Tibetan Buddhist traditions concerning "hidden lands" where people live in peace and happiness, and age extremely slowly. Legend has it that the sun only rises and sets once a year in Hyperborea, which some read literally as referring to the Arctic, but might better be understood as alluding to a Golden Age realm where time is much slower, closer to timelessness than, say, our own hyperfrenetic technological age. The Muses reign there, and it is said to be a land dedicated to Apollo. Pindar, in one of his odes, refers to Hyperborea as inaccessible by ship or by foot, again indicating it as a realm beyond the physical cosmos, yet linked to it. Some sources, relayed by Diodorus Siculus, identify Hyperborea with the island of Britain, and Stonehenge has long been alluded to as Apollo's "circular" temple there.

This kind of mythological symbolism ought not be read too literally. The symbolism of Hyperborea as conveyed by the ancient Greeks and Romans suggests a transcendent origin to the culture that produced the megalithic sites of far Western Europe; and indeed, in perennial philosophy, mathematics is understood as reflecting and revealing the hidden principles informing the cosmos, hierarchically above but reflected in nature. In this respect, and perhaps in others too, mathematics, and in particular sacred geometry, offers insight into the hidden patterns and dimensions within and also beyond the natural world.

When we look at the complex geometry of the almost innumerable megalithic sites of Britain, Scotland, Ireland, Wales, and continental Western Europe, we are compelled to wonder what their purposes were. Why build so many large stone ritual sites? From the perspective of perennial philosophy, there is an answer. The standing stones can be understood as restoring and continuing order in the cosmos, encouraging the cycles of the seasons and weather to remain in balance, keeping the human world safe and flourishing, conveying celestial patterns on earth and in the landscape. In this interpretation, the standing stones of far Western Europe, with their astrological and geometrical intricacies, convey on earth the patterns of heaven, that is, they manifest timelessness in time, and in so doing, can be understood as sustaining the cosmos.

In the Pythagorean-Platonic tradition, number and geometry are seen to inhere in the patterns of the cosmos because they belong to a higher realm, which the physical cosmos reflects and manifests. According to Plato, the human soul and the cosmos have three aspects: the transcendent immaterial, the material, and the intermediate realm between them. What we see in this world, in the shining river through the mountains, in the oceans, in the clouds, in all its beauty, is in the Platonic tradition said to be a reflection of the celestial forms or archetypes that exist in a kind of timelessness. Yet there is more above those celestial archetypes shining in luminous beauty, and that is the transcendence of all images and forms.

This world and "the other"—that of the celestial archetypes—can be conceived of as separate, but they are ultimately one because what exists in time is but a "moving image of eternity." And what joins them is numerical and geometrical pattern, which we see throughout the earth, in the monuments left us from Western great antiquity, and in the celestial patterns of the planets and stars. These could also be understood, metaphorically, as the three worlds of nature, humanity, and the divine. A central purpose of human culture is to recognize the deep mathematical patterns inherent in the cosmos, and to situate them in cultural monuments that manifest them and in doing so, "rectify," balance, and restore the archetypal cosmic patterns of heaven on earth.

One of nature's secrets is that nature needs humanity, needs human reflective awareness expressed in the beauty of cultural creativity, because humanity alone has the capacity to move between the realms, to rebalance and reconfigure what is below so that it reflects what is above. On this world, human consciousness is unique in this role, and that is something unrecognized by those contemporary intellectuals who, looking at the destructive aspects of modern industrial technology, want to condemn all of humanity and extol only wildness on its own without seeing that even if contemporary society largely has lost sight of human possibilities and capacities, perennial philosophy is there to remind us of what our potential is.

A primordial signature of human culture is the stake. Plutarch tells us that Rome was founded from a ploughed circle that no doubt had at its center a stake. From this comes the word "urban," deriving from "orbis," circle, referring to the sacred circle that marks the boundaries of the city. Plutarch remarks, in his "Life of Romulus," that this circle was called *mundus,* world, and corresponded to what is above, the heavens. A stake, pounded into the earth, signifies the axis of the cosmos, the center of worlds, and the uniting of above and below. From the stake, the centerpoint beyond time and space, one can extend a cord, the end of which then can be moved to inscribe a circle. The circumference reflects the sacred circle of the horizon. The same cord, when two other stakes are judiciously placed in the ground, can be used to form a Pythagorean triangle (one right angle [90°]) and two side lengths measuring in whole numbers), that in turn within the circle can mark alignments with the constellations and planets.

The symbolism of these simple geometric forms is profound. The sacred circle extends into space from the timeless center, and with its periphery marks the cyclical passage of time. The stake or axis extends from above to below, and at its base is a point that represents the juncture of time and eternity, the single point of the timeless present moment. The triangles that can be formed within the circle from the stake or center outward mark the relationships between the timeless or unmoving center (eternity) and the moving outward images of the constellations and the planets, that is, the extension of geometrical and numerical patterns "outward" into time and space.

Hence this very simple method—pounding a stake into the ground, extending a knotted cord, marking a circle, and marking triangulated points from the center—represents a cosmic regeneration on the spot, as it were, the emergence of time and space out of timelessness of the beginning (*ab origine*), in the very process of being born (*in statu nascendi*). It marks the *orbis terrarum,* the orb of the earth itself, and the primordial unity between timelessness and time at the beginning of a cycle (the golden age). The ancient symbolism of the dagger/stake, in Sanskrit, *kila,* recapitulates the very moment of creation, the timeless center at the heart of time. And it is significant that the ancient symbolic *kila,* or sacred dagger/stake, carried on in the Tibetan Buddhist tradition from time immemorial, has three sides or blades that come to a point below.

The symbolic language of religious ritual mirrors

nature's language. The purpose of archaic religious ritual is to mirror the ideal patterns of the cosmos, and so to renew it. Timeless is the heart of the ritual that lays out the sacred stones; to enter the sacred stones is to enter into the timelessness out of which the cosmos is ceaselessly born, out of which emerges all order. The stake's or dagger's point symbolizes this timeless center, the vast space out of which time and space continuously appear. And the language of that appearance is numerical and geometrical. Everything in nature bears the imprint of its transcendent origin, because, seen from this perspective, everything is symbol.

The perspective from which everything is symbol is distant from us moderns, for whom everything is object. Seen as an object, everything in nature becomes flat, two-dimensional, something to be exploited. But seen as a symbol, the third dimension, that of the timeless sacred, is restored. What in modernity is just an object to be manipulated, when recognized as a symbol, becomes replete with meaning. And meaning is multivalent; it cannot be reduced to a lower or single level, but instead points toward its own transcendent significance. This is the difference between a bird as an object and a bird as auspicious; this is the difference between the sky and the heavens.

In *Phaedrus,* Plato has Socrates remind us of how one can be transported in the spirit and, as an initiate, see the beauty of the celestial or transcendent archetypes, just as we can also see beauty shining through the natural world. And when we see beauty in nature, in particular in a human face that reminds us of a god or goddess, then we shudder within and feel awe, because, in seeing that natural beauty, we are reminded of transcendent divine beauty. In beatific initiatic vision we are transported to see beauty in its more pure divine forms, but in nature we also can see this transcendent beauty conveyed as if through a glass.

Nature's secret language is symbolic; it reminds us of our and its transcendent origin. Nature has a transparent opacity; its beauty speaks to us because both in us and in it are signs of the transcendent principles of ordered beauty. We recognize those signs in nature because they are there in us as well. The landscape and the sky, the flowing waters and the oceans, the birds and animals and insects, all move us because we feel them in us; we recognize them in us. We are nature's self-awareness, and we are called through that reflective awareness not to exploit nature as a collection of objects and "resources," but to *recognize* nature, to recognize and restore the first principles of beauty and order within nature.

Nature is born anew through our reflective awareness. Only we can regenerate nature by our consciousness; no other being has this capacity. Only we can speak nature's language, and in speaking it, awaken its timeless origin, the transcendent purity out of which it ceaselessly arises. When we see a bird and the bird sees us, when we share consciousness with the bird and the bird's archetypal being, something nearly indescribable has happened that is beyond time and space. What is beyond time and space in nature—that is what calls to us and to nature in us; and it is what is at the heart of the symbolic language of primordial religious ritual.

Perennial philosophy is perennial not because it recurs in time, but because at its center is timelessness. That is what the term "perennial" means at heart. Nature in its magnitude and breathtaking beauty reminds us of timelessness and spacelessness, reminds us of the secret symbolic language that infuses everything in the cosmos, the stars, the planets, the comets and asteroids, the constellations and the clusters and the galaxies, everything. All that is reminds us of what cannot be described as "is" or "is not." That is the secret at the heart of nature's language.

You remember this secret as soon as it is mentioned, don't you? How easy it is to forget it, but the cosmos constantly reminds us, even if we aren't aware of it. Perennial philosophy is not about extracting nature's secrets in order to exploit them; it points rather toward our deepening reflexive awareness of timelessness, our contemplative ascent.

# Chapter Three

# The Contemplative Ascent

Have you not felt, every now and then, the longing to rise up, to fly? It is not for nothing that we dream of having wings. It is a profound metaphor that speaks to something deep and archaic in us. Looking up, when we see a hawk spiraling higher into the empyrean, we rise with it. To begin to realize perennial philosophy is to ascend. But ascent is only one analogy among others, useful for intellectual orientation, yet deceptive when taken too literally. We already encountered the Hermetic axiom "as above, so below," which could in the context of perennial philosophy better be "as within, so without." For "ascent" could better be described as movement inward toward what precedes and transcends not only the senses, but also discursive reason and divided consciousness of self and other.

Although what we are referring to here is not really ascent, still the metaphor is necessary: we need discursive reason to help orient ourselves as we begin to understand more clearly what perennial philosophy really is. Discursive reason is not the enemy, but a friend, a means of orientation as we begin to remember what we have forgotten for so long. Ascent from where to where? you might ask, even as you recognize that we are not thinking of the term in any literal way. Really what we are describing is "movement" from dividedness toward unity, from dualism toward its transcendence. In the sensory world, what we perceive appears to be separate from us, and comes to us through the filters of sight, sound, scent, sensation.

Yet every now and then we experience a point of connection that crosses over the apparent sensory boundary of self and other. Beauty in sight and sound, a delightful fragrance, a loving touch, we all have experienced moments in which we are not entirely separate from another, or from the world around us, moments in which we are carried away, go beyond ourselves, what the ancients called "ecstasy" (ἔκστασις *ekstasis*). In these moments of sensory transcendence, we go beyond ourselves and go beyond our senses, *through* them; our sensory experience becomes a portal into its own transcendence.

The word "ecstasy," though familiar, can be misleading. It derives from *ek-*, or "outside," and *stasis,* sometimes conveyed as "standing," but really meaning "stable condition of being." Ecstasy in this context means that we begin to recognize our own transcendence, that is, the true nature of who we really are, not as a discrete individual, but beyond self-other divisions. When we go into ecstasy, we experience bliss, light, beauty, enduring joy—a blinding purity of reflexive awareness that is immensely pleasurable. We can enter ecstasy through many portals: dance and music, through participation in nature's beauty, through creative activity, through spiritual practices, and through sexual union, to name only a few. Ecstasy means that we begin to leave our provisional or transient self-identity behind and to realize our true nature.

In perennial philosophy, the movement from our discrete individuality (perceived in a sensory context and characterized by an apparent self-other division) toward transcendence is understood as ascent toward perception of the intelligible realm, or of the intelligible. The intelligible abides in itself; it is reflexive self-awareness of itself, and as Plato put it in *Timaeus,* it abides "in its own proper way of life." Intellect is derived from the intelligible; it entails thinking, knowledge of objects/beings that ultimately are not separate from it. The intelligible is beyond being and beings; it is beyond intellect.

But intellect participates in that which it perceives; intellection is participation. Although from a limited sensory perspective, it appears that we perceive objects separate from ourselves, this is true only at the outermost level of experience. As our attention is turned inward and our consciousness ascends, if we may so put it, we also begin to recognize that we participate in beings and beings participate in us; intellection of the intelligible is recognition of what is within us and of what we must be able to recognize as in the continuum of our own field of knowing. We cannot know something entirely outside us that bears no connection to us. The constructions of discursive reason based on the sensory world are merely opinion, but what we are considering here is not opinion. Truth is of a different order of knowledge.

The contemplative ascent is movement from appearance toward reality, and reality is intelligible;

it can be recognized by the intellect. Reality here refers to truth; but truth in this context does not mean *a* truth, but rather that which precedes and transcends all multiplicity, all appearance, all that is dual or dualistic. It is not *a* truth but that which is true; and that which is true endures, it is unchanging and continuous and beyond anything we may say of it. Out of this transcendent reality emerges the intelligible realm, or the intelligibles, out of which in turn is born the cosmos as a moving reflection in time of the living principles beyond it.

Many commonly refer to these living principles as "forms," but the term "forms" is misleading because it is a dead term; it implies that what is above the sensory is somehow two-dimensional or inert. The word "intelligibles" is much better, because it conveys more clearly that which the intellect can recognize, and which possesses a vibrant life and beauty in itself. What is perceived—the intelligible—itself is closer to and participates more purely in that which transcends it, and which is not lesser, but greater reflexive awareness, purer consciousness of consciousness. What the intellect perceives when it approaches the intelligible (if we may so put it) is illumination, transport, purity beyond being.

Plotinus describes this in his incomparable *Enneads,* when he narrates contemplative experience in terms of the rising of the sun. As the sun rises in its splendor over the ocean, it simply gives itself to be seen; and it is of no value to chase after it; one simply waits and experiences its rising. In this experience, we bathe in its light; we are warmed and illuminated, and what we rise toward and experience is not something to be grasped or constructed on our side, but experienced in itself as beyond itself, beyond any thinking or saying, just sheer light and beauty experienced in itself as itself. And ultimately the sun does not rise or set, come or go, but simply is; it has no "whence" but just is.

Here, of course, the sun is also reality, truth, and the unbearable splendor and beauty of truth. And the sun is also a god, Apollo, or Apollo Helios, whose name, Plotinus and others tell us, is *a-pollo,* or *not-manyness,* the god of light and life, of the sun, of prophecy, of truth. We experience the god within us as intelligible, that is, as reality perceptible by us; and this reality is experienced as the overwhelming illumination of light and the warmth and illumination of truth itself. It is also beautiful, even if its beauty is also terrible in its transcendent indifference and blasting light.

And perhaps suddenly you begin to see "polytheism," as the scholars call it, a little differently. For what are these gods of the ancient Greeks or Celts? Did you really think they were like fantasies of schoolchildren, or like divine children, cartoonish? That is what those who recognize only the sensory world and the hegemony of discursive reason would have you believe, perhaps, because that is all that they can muster for themselves. But the reality is a bit different, perennial philosophy tells us. What are these gods? What is a god? A god is a manifestation of the intelligible that serves as a portal for us into higher consciousness.

Because we are far from the polytheistic world,

we might think that a god is entirely separate from us, but that too is not the case. A god is in between sheer transcendence and our human world; if we did not share qualities with the gods, we could not conceive of them or have a rapport with them, or vice versa. It is because they represent aspects of ourselves back to us in alienated form, and awaken those aspects of ourselves, that we belong to the gods. Gods are not human creations, nor are they wholly other; they convey what is above us, and yet also in us. We bear gods within us, and the best of us are godlike.

In Christianity, the celestial hierarchy is conveyed not in polytheistic but in angelic terms, and the master of this tradition is known as Dionysius the Areopagite. Dionysius brought perennial philosophy into Christianity; he served as a conduit, so that the Platonic tradition was conveyed in this new historical stream. In the Dionysian celestial hierarchy, too, the higher spills over into the lower, which in turn serves as initiator for that which is below, so that ultimately all levels of consciousness in the cosmos participate in the transcendent One even if they are not aware of it. And for Dionysius, too, the earthly initiator reflects this same celestial hierarchy; the initiated are dependent upon those who are initiated, who in turn depend upon their own initiators into the transcendent. Dionysius refers to angels, not gods, but one could argue that this is chiefly a matter of nomenclature.

In perennial philosophy, the gods are not to be understood as discrete, separated beings, but as aspects of transcendence that we can realize or convey. The celestial hierarchy for us is fluid in the sense that we can ascend or descend in it according to what we are attracted to. If we are attracted to anger, greed, and ignorance, we can descend; if we are attracted to beauty, generosity, and truth, we can ascend. And what is more, the initiatory hierarchy is really transcendence conveyed from above to below; and initiation does not, in this conception, necessarily require a human initiator; for we can participate in the divine because this is in our intrinsic capacity as human beings. Our initiator might well be an angel or a deity.

In his treatise on one's guardian spirit, Plotinus offers a revealing observation in this regard. This is a section devoted to one's posthumous destiny, one's course of reincarnation. According to Plotinus, after bodily death one inherits the condition that most predominated during one's life. Thus, someone insensate in life may be reborn as a plant; someone who lives a life of the senses along may be reborn as an animal; and someone who lives a life as a god, after death is a god. Who becomes a god after death? Plotinus asks. "Certainly he who was one here," he replies. If one lives one's life according to the spirit above one, then after death, one is freed to be that spirit.

And in his treatise on love, Plotinus tells us how to distinguish between gods and spirits. Although the two terms are often used almost as if they were synonymous, "gods" refers to beings of the intelligible realm, beyond all attachment, existing in radiant freedom, whereas "spirits" refers to beings on this side of the intelligible, those who exist in the hierarchy of the cosmos, some more, others less attached to beings or objects of this world. Hence guardian spirits belong to beings in this world, but gods are not attached to any particular being from the gods' side. The gods abide in the purity and clarity of their own nature.

In "On the Intelligible Beauty," Plotinus has a dazzling passage on what the gods or "watchers" experience in the intelligible realm. "There," he writes, they live the easy life, where all things are transparent, as light is transparent to light; beauty augments beauty; and light augments light; for all "there" is centered in truth perceived by and nourished by pure intellection; to be there is to live in pure wisdom without lack; all there abides in truth and is beautiful; there, exceedingly beautiful watchers observe by the light that pervades them too. Invoking one god is to invoke them all, because each god is all the gods in one.

Damascius serves to clarify Plotinus's remarks a little in his masterwork, *Problems and Solutions Concerning First Principles,* when he points out that we human beings do not experience the intelligible realm directly, in the intellect, but rather (as Plato mentions in his seventh letter) through the "transparent bodies," images, or forms that awaken themselves in us. Hence we can participate indirectly in what the gods and watchers experience directly; and we can do so because we bear within us the intuitive faculty of inner perception that resembles a mirror; we experience the intelligible realm, but we experience it inwardly, in a mediated way.

To purify oneself in order that one become a channel or receptacle for a god or gods, to become a conduit for the god—that, in perennial philosophy, is called "theurgy." The word *theurgy* (θεουργία, *theourgia*) derives from *theo-*(god/divine) and *(en) ergeia,* or work/working. Literally, theurgy means "divine working," or "work of the god." It is the telestic art—meaning the art of final things, ultimately, the art of preparing for the afterlife. Theurgy is purificatory, but it also is apotheotic; both are necessary. The first is the clearing of the soul, and the second is the opening of the soul to the god, the return to the god (*apotheosis*) in keeping with the Platonic *anamnesis,* the remembering of the divine.

There are two complementary aspects of theurgy, one belonging to this world, the other to life after bodily death. With regard to this world, theurgy can be understood as the soul becoming a conduit for the god; the theurgist is one who reveals the god in himself, through ritual praxis, in this way returning the cosmos to the "first day," that is, to the original timelessness out of which time and space emerge. With regard to the next world, the theurgist becomes acclimated to eternity, and so after death will enter into this now familiar timelessness of the gods. Hence theurgy again is the telestic art; it is the art of preparing for death, and as the *Chaldean Oracles* have it, the theurgist is not subject to the "fate of the herds."

In this respect, theurgy is very much akin to Tantric Buddhism. Both Tantric Buddhism and

Greek theurgy make one familiar with the presence of the gods; in their rituals, one enters into timelessness, and embodies the gods. The theurgist recognizes the *sunthemata* (συνθηματα), or transcendent ideas/ archetypes of what we experience in this world; and by recognizing them, the theurgist links together the symbols in this world with their intelligible archetypes, unifying the transcendent and the immanent. The *sunthemata* are the "thoughts of the Father," that is, the transcendent symbols/images that manifest themselves in the "moving images" of the cosmos. By recognizing them, the theurgist returns time to timelessness, if we can so put it. Thus theurgy does not mean rejecting this world, but rather the ritualized returning of it to primordial and archetypal purity. In this, theurgy shares much with Tantrism.

Theurgy, contemplative ascent through symbols and invocation of the gods, is a vital dimension of perennial philosophy. Theurgy means the return of nature to its archetypal and primordial purity; it is the recognition of the paradisal patterns and symbols in the world around us, as much as it is the contemplative ascent through those symbols (*sunthemata*) into the realms of the gods that they reflect both in nature and in us. To put it another way, theurgy is the *via positiva*, the way through images to the transcendence of images.

To see the noetic forms (*theoria*) is to be as a god; it is to perceive the beautiful archetypes of the other realm, but these archetypes are more real than what we see in this world. The gods both contemplate and themselves are (because they participate in) the beautiful noetic ideas that this world reflects. Theurgy is not a separate path from vision (*theoria*); for theurgy is to invoke and evoke the noetic realm out of which the cosmos constantly emerges. It is to participate in the movement from timelessness into time, and from time into timelessness; it is to participate in the perpetual moment of creation.

All great art is theurgic. Great poetry is liturgic; when we enter into its spell, we are brought into a higher and more profound consciousness. The lines of great poetry bring us closer to eternity; to hear or read living poetry is to be exalted. Great poetry is so because it invokes and evokes beauty and truth beyond itself. So too mythopoetic visual art: its proportions, its geometry are perfect, but beyond this it is invested with an otherworldly beauty, so we see through it into a more exalted realm and consciousness. All great art exalts us. Both the maker and the audience are raised up by what is conveyed through the work, through the song, through the myth, through the image. Great art is both perfected and perfecting.

And why does great art exalt us? Art unifies the observer and that which is observed; its beauty transports us beyond our customary doubleness and division into a union with what we see and hear. But there is more, for we also unite with what the artwork reminds us of. All great art recalls to us our own celestial memories, our nostalgia for otherworldly beauty; it reminds us of paradise. Paradise is familiar to us from the past and from the future, because it does not belong to the time of this world. When we experience great art, it comes to us redolent with the scents of paradise; its beauty is eerie for its otherworldliness, and we can never quite discern why.

Authentic and living literary, musical, and visual arts all awaken in us celestial memories; they recall eternity to us, and in their austere and perfect beauty, they remind us of what transcends us. This is the standard by which all the arts are judged; for art without mystery is not art at all, only stimulation by sound or sight. And if art is ugly, dissonant, perverse, if it does not remind us of our celestial home, but only provides a gimcrack in this one, then it is not art at all, is it? Perennial philosophy is perennial because its reference point is transcendent eternity; and it provides us with a natural understanding of why we feel what we feel in the presence of greatness.

All authentic art is spiritual; to experience it is only different in kind from religious ritual because it is more individual. But to experience a great poem, to see a great painting, to hear a great work of music, is to feel awakening in us what also awakens in living religious ritual—it is as if a light is kindled in us; we are illuminated by these in the same way, because all authentic art is ultimately religious.

Theurgy is a more concentrated form of religious ritual, intensified and purified in order to achieve particular aims, above all, to establish special exaltation in the theurgist, to bring one out of ordinary consciousness and into the divine awareness that we also can experience after death. Perennial philosophy reminds us that what we experience after death, we cultivated in ourselves in this life. When we are surrounded by great art, when we listen to exalting music, when we hear exalted poetry, we are establishing ourselves more firmly in an afterlife of which these are evocations and reflections.

Contemplative ascent is akin to what we experience in great art, and to what we experience when we are exalted by being in a profoundly beautiful place in nature, high in the mountains, overlooking the ocean, wherever the sense of spaciousness expands our awareness beyond ourselves. All our contemplative experiences are akin to one another, and theurgy is another word for orchestrating them, for bringing together lyrics and music, rhythm and scent, landform and temple, concentrating them into a special kind of exaltation.

For behind and within all of these is infused sacred number, sacred geometry, sacred patterns and rhythms that inhere in the cosmos and that point us toward its transcendent origin. In vowels and consonants, in sound and sight and scent, in the living moment of religious ritual, we are called neither to the past nor to the future, but to eternity. All great art and all living religious ritual reminds us of what we can be, of a still distant deification that nonetheless we know instinctively is ours. The contemplative ascent is not only to the heart of the cosmos, but beyond it into what we can only describe by negation. The *via positiva* goes through the beauty of images and sounds and scents, but it is completed in what transcends all of these.

# Chapter Four

# Transcendence

At the heart of perennial philosophy is absolute transcendence. From Plato through Plotinus to Damascius, one finds recurrent the recognition that above intellection, above intellect, behind all thought and perception is the transcendence of these. This transcendence Plotinus called "the One," meaning by that what is beyond intellect and knowledge, totally ineffable and beyond all dualities. But really, this transcendence is also beyond the concept of "the One," because as Plotinus himself puts it, it has no name, and we cannot capture it in words or concepts.

We can use the term "above," but even that kind of vertical terminology is misleading, because what we are considering here, at the heart of perennial philosophy, cannot be fully expressed verbally or conceptually. Rather, this transcendence can be expressed only parabolically, by gestures or by negation, by turning words or concepts against themselves. Thus, for instance, Plotinus tells us in "On the Knowing Hypostasis" that although we can say something about it, we cannot directly speak it, and do not have knowledge of it. We can say what it is not, but not what it is; we can divine the One as that which is higher than being, greater than anything that may be said about it, but we cannot accurately convey it.

Those who claim perennial philosophy is dualistic manifestly do not understand it, and are not familiar with it or its metaphysics. Even the term "non-dual" is dubious, because "non-dual," while perhaps in some respects accurate, is misleading because it is an assertion against dualism, and the transcendence we are discussing here cannot be captured in the term "non-dual" either. Without doubt, perennial philosophy has at its center absolute simplicity and absolute transcendence; this much is clear throughout the entire Platonic tradition.

In Plato's dialogues, we find this transcendence in *Parmenides,* where Socrates and Parmenides discuss how above the realm of ideas is absolute knowledge of the One, which cannot be understood through discursive reason, but only indicated by way of negation. The contemplative ascent through the archetypal realm to absolute transcendence is indicated in *Parmenides,* itself recapitulating this ascent. We also find it indicated near the end of *Timaeus,* where we find an extended discussion of uncreated and indestructible being, always the same, invisible, inaccessible to the senses, like space, timeless, and perceptible by contemplative intelligence.

Plotinus devotes considerable effort to analyze the nature of that which is beyond existence and beyond self-sufficiency, beyond any discursive thoughts that might be applied to it. He remarks on how the discursive reason wants to consider one thing after another, methodically, but how it cannot approach the absolutely simple. The intellect can perceive it, but during the perception it cannot speak about it, and afterward has difficulty conveying what it experienced. Transcendence is experienced as light; illumination alone is sufficient for the soul, whose true purpose is to experience illumination not by another light that is external, but by the very light of consciousness which is its own self-perception. How could this happen? Plotinus asks. "Take away everything!" he replies.

In another treatise, "What is Beyond Being Does Not Think," Plotinus continues his exposition of transcendence. In thinking, there is always doubleness: there is the thinker and that which is thought. A thought of a horse, or of righteousness, is implicitly dual. But in the Good, that is, in transcendence, there is no duality; there is only the Good as Good, which does not need thinking because thought is characteristic of that which is aspiring, and the Good does not aspire, nor does it think, because it is sufficient in itself to itself. What is beyond being is also beyond thinking; it is beyond the reach of discursive reason.

Transcendence is also a primary theme of Damascius, the last head of the Platonic Academy. In his masterwork, much of his effort is spent on discursive analysis of transcendence, much as in Plotinus, with a special emphasis on carefully describing the experience of transcendence. Damascius points us toward absolute and primary knowledge of what he terms the intelligible, "the supermundane abyss." We comprehend the intelligible not by approaching it as something other, not by seeking to appropriate it into ourselves, but by simplification of our consciousness so that we can apprehend it. As the *Chaldean Oracles* put it, one extends "an empty mind toward the intelligible in order to comprehend it." Through concentration of the mind, one enters into the undifferentiated nature of the intelligible, experiencing directly the luminous cognition of transcendence.

In his *magnum opus, Problems and Solutions Concerning First Principles,* and especially in "On the One and On Knowledge of the One," Damascius writes that our "unitary knowledge" comes not from the duller faculty of ratiocination, but through intuitive and immediate cognition, opening the flower of our cognition toward the transcendent. Of course, strictly speaking, the One cannot be known because it is neither knowable nor not knowable; it does not belong to the realm of objects and subjects and thus cannot become an object of knowledge. Rather, it, and the Ineffable that is beyond being and beyond the One, cannot be grasped by discursive reason or through conceptualizations, but only can be intuited; that is, what corresponds to this transcendence in us, we can directly realize. The transcendent is undifferentiated and beyond all things or being; and even to attempt to define or analyze it is to obscure it.

The elusive nature of transcendence in Platonism is quite important. We find this elusiveness in Plato's dialogues, as well as in Plotinus's *Enneads,* and much of Damascius's masterwork also concerns this topic. It is important because it is almost never remarked upon, yet is vital to understanding the real nature both of Platonism and of perennial philosophy more broadly. Genuinely understanding Platonism and perennial philosophy means recognizing that these are not only cosmological traditions; perennial philosophy has metaphysical implications in the sense of *ta meta ta physica,* that is, what goes beyond or transcends the cosmos and/or the physical world and physics. And what transcends this is the Ineffable, the transcendent center of perennial philosophy. That we can experience this transcendence is central to the greater meaning of perennial philosophy: to experience transcendence is to be liberated from time/space and subject/object imprisonment.

This theme of transcendence can be traced into Christianity, just as it can be found also later in Sufism in Islam and Kabbalah in Judaism. Exoteric monotheisms are marked by insistence on doctrinal belief systems based in a radical dualism of believer/ external deity, but nonetheless bear within them a perennial philosophy, introduced in the case of Christianity by Dionysius the Areopagite. In our overview here, we will concentrate on Christianity because our broader focus is on perennial philosophy in Western Anglo-European tradition.

Still, it bears mentioning not only that Christianity, Islam, and Judaism have included esoteric Platonic traditions, but also that the kind of transcendence being discussed here bears a marked resemblance to *shunyata* or emptiness in Buddhism. One also finds an emphasis on transcendence in Vedanta, of course, though it is more along the lines of a posited identity of the individual self with a transcendent Self, whereas Buddhism emphasizes the emptiness of the self (*anatman*) too. And when we look at perennial philosophy as it appeared in the seminal works of Dionysius the Areopagite in early Christianity, just as in Platonism, what we find is closest to Buddhist emptiness.

The most definitive early text for all of Christian mysticism is the *Mystical Theology* attributed to Dionysius the Areopagite. We do not know who Dionysius was, and it is telling that some have attributed the Dionysian *corpus* to various Platonists, including Damascius. Were the Dionysian works actually written by a Platonist or Platonists in order to convey the essential Platonic tradition into Christianity? It certainly would seem so. And in any event, what we find in the *Mystical Theology* is the inception of a Platonic tradition within Christianity that would carry forward for centuries upon centuries.

Dionysius's treatise on the celestial hierarchy provided Christianity with what we have termed the contemplative ascent, as well as the concept of initiation, but the most essential element provided by Dionysius is in his treatise on the mystical theology, and in particular on the nature of transcendence. In *Mystical Theology,* Dionysius urges the reader toward the diligent exercise of mystical contemplation in which one leaves behind the senses and the operations of the intellect, and all things sensible and intellectual, and all things in the world of being and nonbeing, so that we may attain that which transcends all being and all knowledge.

This transcendence Dionysius describes as a dazzling Mystery wherein one moves into pure and transcendent silence and illumination so intense that it is a kind of darkness. Those who are attached to the objects of thought, or to their own concepts and beliefs, cannot reach such understanding; they remain uninitiated. But the judicious reader is called to realize a Darkness beyond light, and, without seeing and without knowing, to see and to know that which is above vision and knowledge. This transcendence has no body or form, shape, quality, or quantity; it has no being or non-being; it is not essence, or eternity, or time; it cannot be described as wisdom or power or truth; it is neither false nor true; it is beyond every negation or descriptor.

To trace this theme of transcendence after Dionysius would take a volume in itself; but most important is that Dionysius provided an authoritative touchstone for those who came after him. Those who discovered *Mystical Theology* had immediate access to the most precious insight of Platonism, the nature of which had been elaborated by Plotinus and Damascius, but in Dionysius's work, it was condensed into a slim, pure, portable form. It recurs in numerous medieval works; it is at the center of John Scotus Eriugena's *Periphyseon;* it is there at the center of Meister Eckhart's extraordinary sermons and treatises; it is visible in works like *The Cloud of Unknowing;* it is present in the early modern era in what Jacob Böhme and John Pordage called the unground and the nothing; in the nineteenth century, we can glimpse it in the mystical experience related by Ralph Waldo Emerson in his first book, *Nature;* and it is certainly present in the works of the great twentieth-century Russian philosopher Nicholas

Berdyaev. In fact, it is visible in the work that you are reading right now.

But what matters here is not genealogical. And what matters here is not comparative. What matters here is transcendence. By this I mean that there was very clearly a deep divide between Platonism and Christianity during the early Christian period, and the fiercest polemics by Christians against Platonism were by those who most insisted on a dualistic belief system in which the individual man petitioned (is subject to and "permanently" separate from) a monotheistic god. This is why Porphyry and other Platonists, and the Emperor Julian too, were intensely critical of the Christianity that came to the fore during this period: they recognized how much was at stake.

Because the Platonic cosmology and metaphysics is all of a piece, an organic whole, it provides a way to understand the human being as part of and reflecting the cosmic order, and also as able to ascend toward self-transcendence. Admittedly, through Dionysius the Areopagite, and through the subsequent Christian mystics, Platonism did have at least a foothold in the Christian tradition, just as it to some extent can be found in Sufism in Islam, in Kabbalah in Judaism, in Manichaeism and in other religious currents as well. But an intrinsic opposition exists in monotheism between those who insist on exoteric, dualistic perspectives characterized by belief, and those who champion more esoteric perspectives that point toward self-other transcendence.

Transcendence is the key. There are distinctions to

be made here, of course. There is a difference between the kind of transcendence one finds in Vedanta, for instance, in which the self (*atman*) is ultimately identical with transcendence (*Brahman*), but the transcendence is understood in terms of self; and the kind of transcendence one finds in Buddhism, in which self (and other) are understood as emptiness. What we see in Platonism has elements of both of these, though our primary sources, especially Plotinus and Damascius, suggest that it may be closer in the end to Buddhism. Certainly the Christian mystical tradition from Dionysius through Eckhart and *The Cloud of Unknowing* seems very analogous to Mahayana Buddhism and the sheer transcendence that we also see in the Heart of Perfect Wisdom Sutra.

But regardless of such comparative distinctions, perennial philosophy is perennial because of transcendence. By this I mean that even if a cosmology and metaphysics based in transcendence is anathematized, nonetheless, experiences of transcendence do not disappear as a result; since a capacity for self-transcendence is part of what it means to be human, individuals will continue to rediscover it. Perennial philosophy is rediscovered and reconstituted in a new cultural context as soon as the core ideas emerge. And at the center of those core ideas is transcendence.

Transcendence here means an individual is not strictly only an individual, but opens up into what is beyond the individual, beyond the subject/object dichotomy.

Human possibility is far greater than is sometimes assumed, and the basis of human possibility is openness to transcendence, which is central to ritual, to poetry, to the arts, to dance, to song, to myth and legends, to culture and to religion at once. Transcendence includes ecstasy, or enstasy, whichever word one might prefer, in either case meaning that one goes beyond "self."

Great poets understand this intuitively. One sees it in the poetry of Rainer Maria Rilke, especially his *Sonnets to Orpheus* and *Duino Elegies;* one sees it in the poems of T. S. Eliot, whose greatest work turns on precisely this moment of transcendence, the still point of the turning world; and Ezra Pound understood it too, observing once in an aside that the flavors of the peach and the apricot are not lost from one generation to the next, nor are they transmitted by book learning. Likewise, he said, mystical insight is also dependent on direct perception, a knowledge as permanent as the faculty for perceiving it. And W. B. Yeats was familiar with it too, as was the poet H.D., and, of course, Kathleen Raine, the last Romantic.

What these poets all perceived intuitively is what is inherent not only in Platonism, but beyond Platonism in perennial philosophy that is visible too in the poetic tradition of Orphism, where Platonism has its roots. We will recall that Orpheus, the legendary poet and musician; the theurge/magus who charmed the beasts and who went into the underworld after Eurydice; the founder of the Orphic Mystery rites, whose mournful singing charmed even the god of death himself; that Orpheus was torn apart by

Thracian Maenads (or in another version, was struck by lightning by Zeus) and his head and lyre famously floated down the river, still singing mournful songs. The symbolism here is obvious: the body torn apart, the severed head, the consciousness not limited to a body or a self, but transcending limitations, bringing the mysteries of the gods to humanity.

The symbolism of Orpheus's death is akin to that of Actaeon torn apart by the hounds of Diana: the self is transcended and in that transcendence is a different kind of immortality, entry into eternity, the timelessness of the gods. Hence also the moving beauty of Orpheus's songs/poems, which are accompanied by the lyre, by the tuned strings of cosmic harmonization, the Pythagorean chords that restore celestial order to the cosmos. Orpheus's music is magical and mystical at once: it is telestic, symbolized by an image that at first may seem grotesque—the singing head and playing lyre upon the waters—but that actually conveys in itself both the contemplative ascent to the divine realm and transcendence; it conveys divinization.

To understand the symbolic language of the ancients, one must not take it literally; it is always anagogical. What Dionysius the Areopagite wrote about symbolic language can be applied to understanding more ancient myths and sagas as well: even the most apparently grotesque or dissonant image, understood properly, is the right way to convey a particular meaning about the divine that cannot be conveyed in any other way. When Plato writes about divine madness, the term conveys the leaving behind of ordinary self-other consciousness and entering into a new kind of awareness.

One of the central problems for moderns in understanding perennial philosophy is that we no longer think anagogically; we do not understand how to read myths because we tend to interpret everything literally. Fundamentalist literalism is symptomatic of our time, but scientific rationalists are little different, for nearly everyone is inclined toward a privileging of self and of discursive reason, sometimes overcome by emotionalism. But the ancient mysteries were conveyed anagogically, through symbols, because they are beyond both discursive reason and distorting emotional reactions. And the greatest of these mysteries was transcendence of the self.

Transcendence is not opposed to reason. It cannot be grasped through discursive reason, of course, but in Plotinus's and Damascius's work we see that it can be carefully analyzed and indicated by negation or by symbols and parables, alluded to, presented in inventive ways. Reason is a great gift, but we sometimes think it can take us where it cannot. Perennial philosophy offers so many different indications of what transcendence is, in various contexts and traditions, according to the personalities of those who present it. But always, in the end, transcendence remains beyond whatever is said.

Nonetheless, and despite the elusiveness of all descriptions, indications, or symbols, transcendence of subject-object duality is the center and turning-point of perennial philosophy. Human beings have an intrinsic capacity for transcendence; it is a perception of the fundamental nature of reality itself. And although ways of indicating it vary, this does not mean that therefore there are multiple natures of reality. There aren't. Rather, we benighted folks, caught in the incessant nattering of our discursive reason, pulled this way and that by our greed or aversion, by the clouding of emotional reactions, nonetheless can perceive the transcendent nature of reality. The enduring purpose of perennial philosophy is to remind us that this is possible. To its implications for human culture we now turn.

# Chapter Five

# Above and Below

Perennial philosophy is all too often misunderstood. Among misunderstandings is the notion that perennial philosophy results from comparison, as though it derived from the superimposition of multiple religions and the acceptance of what they might have in common. But that kind of view, however prevalent, is incorrect. Rather, as we have seen, perennial philosophy is fundamentally experiential in nature, and reflects the recognition that a contemplative ascent is possible for us human beings, and further, that realization of transcendence is also possible. Perennial philosophy holds that there is a central path to transcendence, and that we find this path reflected in different religious traditions without being limited to any one of them. But there is more—for this individual path also has cultural implications.

To understand the cultural implications of perennial philosophy, we will stay with the Platonic tradition that has been our lodestone during this journey. But there is another Western tradition that also will be useful to us here, and that is the tradition of Hermes. Hermetism and Platonism actually belong to a shared world in antiquity; they offer different insights into the same underlying perennial philosophy. Hermes is the god of communication and divine revelation; Hermes, the wingéd god, ascends and descends, and one of his watchwords was "as above, so below," the first assertion in the mysterious text known as the *Tabula Smaragdina,* or *The Emerald Tablet of Hermes.*

*The Emerald Tablet of Hermes* is found in numerous versions, some in Latin, others in Arabic, and it is most well known for its application in alchemy, the art of transmutation. But for us, the *Emerald Tablet* has a different significance: it shows us perennial philosophy applied. This concise set of aphorisms originates in a cave, as a revelation there to us from Hermes. It begins with the affirmation that what is above corresponds to what is below, but what is more, both above and below are united in the One. The One is inherent in all things; all things emerge from the One, or are adaptations of it. The *Tablet* goes on to say that its father is the sun, its mother is the moon, the wind carries it, and the earth nurses it. It is the progenitor of all "works of wonder" (*telesmi*) in the world, and its power is integral or complete. It ascends above and descends below; it is the glory of the cosmos, and, the strength of strength, it penetrates everything, subtle and solid. It is the work of the Sun. And with that *The Emerald Tablet* concludes.

We can better understand this seminal text in light of perennial philosophy, which it certainly reflects. The *Emerald Tablet* begins with the assertions that what is above is also below, and that all things originate in the One. This is a highly condensed version of what we discussed already in much more detail: first, that in perennial philosophy there is a hierarchy that stretches from below to above, from the physical to the supraphysical to the transcendent. And second, that there is a transcendent origin to all phenomena, which here, as in Plotinus, is termed "the One." This is a cosmological text: it primarily concerns the One's inherence in all phenomena, and as is clear in Damascius, the One is in part a way of conceiving how the cosmos emerges out of transcendence (what Damascius refers to as the main problem of first principles).

The *Tablet* is not only about how the cosmos emerges out of the One, but also about how the One inheres in the cosmos—how it is the child of the sun and moon, how the wind carries it, how the earth nourishes it, how its power is integral and complete, how it penetrates everything solid and subtle. All of these refer to the One as inherent in all things, and as the strength of all strength, that is, the essence of vitality and life itself. The One is not to be understood as separate from this world, any more than what is above is to be understood as "somewhere else." Naturally, then, the One also is the source of magic, wonders, the perfecting of phenomena (*telesmi*). This perfecting can also be understood as "the work of the Sun," Sun here, as in Plotinus, being anagogic for the One.

The *Emerald Tablet*, a highly condensed version of perennial philosophy, is primarily cosmological and alchemical. It is about how transcendence is inherent in immanence, and about how we human beings can transmute and reveal the hidden perfection within nature. It is theurgic, to use the Platonic term. Alchemy is the work of perfecting nature; it is working with nature in order to reveal not only the essences, but ultimately the transcendence within it. Yet alchemy is nonetheless primarily cosmological; it even could be described as applied transcendence. Alchemy is also applied Hermetism.

Hermetism is a branch of perennial philosophy with deeper cultural implications than usually recognized. And it is the cultural implications of perennial philosophy that concern us now. Contemplative ascent and transcendence are individual matters, but there are wider and deeper cultural significances to them. To see inwardly the beauty of the ideas that inform the cosmos, to connect with the gods, and to attain some direct realization of transcendence, all of these signify wisdom.

We have not referred much to wisdom as yet, but its connection to these other topics should be obvious. Wisdom is the crown of the contemplative ascent and realization; from the cultural perspective, it is their purpose and meaning. To honor the gods means to honor the principles that they represent, and to incarnate those principles in oneself. To worship or honor the gods is to become like them, and to convey them into the world. And as to transcendence, that is the font of wisdom itself. Transcendence in this context means freedom from the self-other or subject-object dichotomy; it is the very basis for injunctions to care for others. We care for others because fundamentally, we and they are united by the substratum of transcendence that inheres in everything in the cosmos.

We need to recognize how perennial philosophy provides a metaphysical context for understanding wisdom within a culture. In contemporary society, there really is no context for wisdom. We are familiar with the word, but what does it really mean? We do not know. In the context of perennial philosophy, however, wisdom is the natural result of realizing transcendence of self-other dualism. The contemplative is not an escapist, but rather the individual in society who is most intent upon awakening into and manifesting truth; wisdom is a term for a result of that awakening. In the context of perennial philosophy, the word "sage" refers to someone who has experienced this process of awakening to truth.

But of course, now we are entering into a whole area that seems to be off limits to moderns, because it raises a great many uncomfortable questions or issues. Since our subject is cultural applications of perennial philosophy, however, we need to delve into this largely unmapped territory as well. At heart, perennial philosophy is an individual path of contemplative ascent and realization, as we have seen, yet nonetheless it has social and cultural implications. In ancient Rome, some of these implications were recognized, which is why one sees really extraordinary philosopher-kings like Marcus Aurelius or Julian, who were trained and counseled by philosophers, and indeed were themselves philosophers.

While the metaphysics and cosmology of perennial philosophy exist to some extent independently of the particular society in which the individual practitioner lives, one does have to ask how perennial philosophy might be applied within a society, and when one does, one inevitably comes to the concept of a spiritual aristocracy who are entrusted with the training of others who come to exemplify it too. And from the concept of a spiritual aristocracy one then comes to the idea of educational institutions meant to foster and further perennial philosophy. Often such institutions are relatively informal, as appears to have been the case with the various Platonic Academies.

This is true of the Platonic Academies in antiquity, for the most part, and it is also true of Hermetic groups, as also of subsequent groups not only in the medieval period, like practitioners of *via negativa* mysticism, but also of the Renaissance group around Marsilio Ficino, and for that matter, of the American Transcendentalists of the nineteenth century, in particular those in the ambit of Ralph Waldo Emerson and Bronson Alcott and in the Concord School of Philosophy.

It is of course true that perennial philosophy is transmitted through writing—as we see from Plato and Plotinus onward to Emerson—and so it is possible to rediscover earlier writings and reconstitute perennial philosophy from them in a new environment. That is effectively what Emersonian Transcendentalism is. The Concord School of Philosophy was a fledgling subsequent attempt to develop an informal academy. It was, however, not clearly enough centered on Platonism or mysticism (though those topics certainly appeared in the proceedings), and it never really constituted a hatchery for practitioners of perennial philosophy.

And indeed, the idea of philosophical counsel to prospective leaders—let alone the notion of leaders themselves being philosophers—seems quite remote from most contemporary political practices. The process of elections in representative or parliamentary democracies generally is grueling and relentless for candidates, who rarely have a moment to think, let alone seek wise counsel; and in any event the counsel proffered largely concerns gaining largesse from wealthy contributors, or in catering to particular interest groups. As a result, the leaders one sees in modern societies often seem to have been selected for venality rather than for principles, and for ambition for power rather than for the long-term good of the people, let alone for wisdom.

All the same, one has to ask whether it is really so inconceivable that leaders be selected for wisdom. That is another implication of the adage in the *Tablet* "as above, so below." Obviously, contemplative practice and transcendence is the center of perennial philosophy as we've considered it so far, and these both concern the individual realizing transcendence. However, ideally, there should be ways for that individual path to be expressed socially, if it were to begin to influence society directly. That was the purpose of the philosophical training of exceptional imperial Romans, examples of which include Marcus Aurelius and Julian.

And this is why one finds a consistent connection in the Platonic tradition between the philosophical path, educational training groups or organizations to support and continue that path, and guidance for prospective leaders. We see this in Plato's *Republic,* which is really a kind of thought experiment on the part of the speakers about what a state might look like were it guided by a philosophical path. Like so much of Plato's work, the *Republic* is an indicative work, allusive and coy. We also see the political-social application of Platonism in *Laws,* where once again the underlying idea is how one might create a state that best reflects and encourages enduring principles and the quest for philosophical wisdom.

Such an idea also impelled Plotinus to propose to the Roman emperor Gallienus and his wife Salonina that a philosophical community called "Platonopolis" be developed in Campania. Plotinus and his associates (including both men and women) initially would have guided this philosophical community, which would have been an opportunity to restore a legendary "city of philosophers." Although the plan did not come to fruition, the very existence of the proposal demonstrates that even so metaphysical and contemplative a figure as Plotinus recognized what Plato also had seen, that the philosophical path ought to influence society and society's leaders more broadly.

Such a proposal for a philosophically guided community ultimately entails developing a philosophical culture. Here, as is obvious, the word "philosophical" refers to the contemplative ascent, and not to combative exhibitions of discursive reason. We know that it is possible for a philosophically guided community or even a nation to exist in the contemporary world because we have the example of the kingdom of Bhutan, a tiny land in the Himalayas whose wise young ruler, guided by Buddhism, encouraged his people to aspire not to ever-greater "gross domestic product" (GDP) but rather to ever-greater "gross domestic happiness" (GDH). Measuring one's success in this way is, of course, a philosophical experiment with numerous implications; and to make it real requires that there be an entire culture supporting it.

A culture guided by perennial philosophy would have recognizable characteristics, and we see some of them in Bhutan. Such a culture is guided by wisdom, which is to say, knowledge and compassion. Knowledge is necessary to guide one above—it provides a map for the contemplative ascent—and the correlate application of above to below, the application of spirituality in culture is an expression of compassion, not only to other human beings, but also to birds, animals, plants, and the land and waters. A philosophical culture is humane because it expresses and encourages what is best in us; it is an expression of and an encouragement to the realization of truth, beauty, and goodness in ourselves.

If we live in a debased world, it is perhaps rather easy to dismiss a perennial culture as a pipe dream. If we are threatened by violence; if the society we live in is callous toward birds, animals, plants, land, and waters; if the people we see are venal and greedy and aggressive; if the buildings we see and live in are ugly; if the art we see is fragmented and grotesque;

if people are inculcated with nihilism and relativism; if even the apparent élite seem lost; it would not be surprising were a perennial culture to seem impossibly far off.

But how things seem often blinds us to what can be. What can we observe about a perennial culture? First, it cannot be too large. Plotinus's vision was for a single city, Platonopolis, and that seems about right, though the example of Bhutan suggests that a larger geographical area would be feasible, providing there is a history of linguistic and religious continuity across the land. Second, the relatively small community must have an inclination to share; there must be a common spirit. There would likely need to be some degree of genetic connection; history would suggest that most conflicts come from aggression of one disparate group against another. Third, such a culture must have a shared aspirational center, a collective aspiration to encourage realization of truth, beauty, and goodness to the degree possible.

And so, a thought experiment: imagine, if you will, your own such community. What would it look like? How large would it be? The very diversity of the possibilities is a testimony to perennial philosophy. At the center of such a community are common aspirations, yet the expression depends very much on the ambience and the participants, on all the innumerable variables that produce this result and not that, this kind of cultural expression and not that. And yet within the disparate possibilities is a perennial center, visible in the contemplative ascent and in the affirmation of transcendence, however these might be culturally expressed.

The ideal community might well be a group that gathers around a master or teacher. That was certainly the model for the Platonists, who typically were themselves taught by a master, as Plotinus was by Ammonius Saccas. Pythagoras, Plato, Plotinus, each had a circle around them, and one wants to restore the word "cult" to its original and purer meaning of a group devoted to spiritual practice and aspiration. The pejorative use of "cult," with all its sinister associations, is a modern inversion of an vitally important earlier meaning. A charismatic leader, a group of disciples with shared aspirations, these can be either the worst or the best. Corruptio optimae pessima. What in the contemporary world may be a grotesque parody or a tragedy nonetheless does not gainsay the value and meaning of the original.

At heart, this community is a kind of spiritual family, whose parents raise children who, when grown, in turn themselves raise children. The spiritual family is the heart of the perennial culture, whose root, one cannot but acknowledge, is *cult*. Cult is part of the same linguistic family that gives us *cultivate,* and *agriculture*—the words all share the idea of raising, nurturing, caring for, producing through human art. In this regard, "as above, so below" conveys a sense that ideally such a community reflects and manifests below what is above, the life of the gods, serene, joyous, filled with beauty, goodness, and truth. That this is easily dismissed and ridiculed by the cynic as a Cloudcuckooland, or for that matter, parodied by a type of sociopath does not eliminate the possibility of a virtuous original.

In truth, such a group, a cult, is the natural form by which the perennial culture is created and sustained. Numerous such groups, in different areas of life, some expressly devoted to religion, others devoted to agriculture or metalworking or the arts of the warrior, some to poetry and song, or to crafts, some to hunting, fishing, or navigation, others to engineering and building, together form the tapestry of a culture as a whole. Out of such groups come guilds and other communities both informal and formal, which shape a culture's artistic expression in all walks of life.

This kind of natural cultural organization happens spontaneously even today; it happens whenever a community with a spiritual center emerges, and it no doubt will continue to happen in the future precisely because it is perennial, that is, recurring naturally whenever the conditions are ripe for it. But for it to flourish, as Peter Kingsley pointed out, a culture must be tended; it needs guardians and sages, protectors who can shape and guide it. What we are describing in this little book is not only perennial philosophy as an individual process, but also perennial philosophy as it is expressed culturally.

We saw earlier that perennial philosophy can be described as movement out of the cave into the light of day, and what we are describing here is the second part of that allegory of the cave, when the former cave dweller returns to the cave in order to convey to the truth to those still trapped therein. Culture can be described as how we convey that truth; culture expresses the contemplative ascent and transcendence in diverse ways, to be sure, but ultimately its message is that we can ascend, that we can attain higher understanding, that we can move toward divine knowledge and wisdom.

In great antiquity, this ascent was symbolized very simply and beautifully in the forms that stretched from below to above, be they megaliths, natural stone outcroppings like the *Externsteine,* or Greek or Roman columns. Through architecture and through recognition and shaping of particular naturally occurring forms like stones, caves, hills, and mountains, the cultures of Anglo-Europe expressed themselves, and in this expression demonstrated the movement from below to above, and from above to below. Such movement is what we term culture.

# Chapter Six

# Contemplative Science

Although we have been using the term "perennial philosophy" consistently, and although in fact this book is an explication of perennial philosophy pure and simple, nonetheless at this point we might remark that another term for what we have been describing—and probably a better one—is "contemplative science." The term "contemplative science" has much to recommend it, not the least of which is that it conveys more precisely than "perennial philosophy" itself its defining features, namely contemplative ascent and transcendence. What is more, it conveys very well the union of what often seem to be two distinct and opposed approaches, the contemplative, and the scientific.

Of course, most of us take for granted that the contemplative and the scientific spheres are, always have been, and always will be separate and even opposed to one another. And in fact this division is quite self-perpetuatingly "real," for inasmuch as we accept any (con)temporary definitions of contemplation and science as separate and/or opposed, then they are in fact so. And after all, what passes for "mysticism" in the popular parlance is typically any old thing, for falling down in a fit, hallucinations, trance, stigmata, visions, and other phenomena may end up in that vague category. At the same time, "science" is often (despite the development of speculative physics) popularly characterized in materialistic and certainly ratiocentric terms. And there is some truth in the opinion that never the twain (if seen as *this* twain) shall meet.

But actually, both of these are mischaracterizations. There is, or at least, should be no opposition between contemplative practice as we have been describing it and scientific exploration. In fact, the two fit together perfectly well. The contemplative ascent and transcendence described in Plotinus's *Enneads,* and the metaphysics of Damascius are in their respective works outlined matter-of-factly and with every effort to develop logical consistency and precision. The term "contemplative science" is certainly appropriate for a figure like Plotinus, and for the Pythagorean-Platonic tradition more broadly, because these authors sought to delineate not an idiosyncratic vision but rather the nature of the cosmos, the contemplative ascent, and transcendence, as they perceived them in their own inner experience.

The difference is that contemporary scientific exploration focuses primarily on understanding what is without rather than what is within. By and large, scientists have been concerned with external laws or functions, external causes and effects, and not with the inner life of the mind. Only very recently has neuroscience and cognitive science begun to peer into the possibilities of inner or spiritual life, and even so, has largely remained on the far periphery, concerned with the rough aspects of human consciousness, with raw emotional reactions like fear or anger, and only infrequently if at all with contemplative practices, let alone contemplative ascent, or transcendence.

But scientific approaches are quite compatible with contemplative introspection or experience: both seek to investigate phenomena, to form a more coherent understanding of them, to formulate a theoretical framework for understanding the cosmos and human beings, and to develop an understanding of universally applicable truths. Of course, contemplative introspection seeks not only truths, but also truth. In principle, such a goal is not in conflict with science, which also seeks the truth. The difference is in method. Science, as widely understood, is not about the existential transmutation or awakening of the individual to truth; rather, it is about the unveiling of hidden laws or mechanisms governing external phenomena, with an eye to practical applications.

Contemplative science, on the other hand, by its very nature requires the existential awakening of the individual; to know truth, one has to come to see and to realize it for oneself. One's mind has to be suitable for recognizing it; it has to become a suitable vessel. Contemplative science is thus the existential transformation of the individual; the seer has to be capable of being or recognizing that it is the seen. Contemplative introspection is, obviously, a very different process than the discursive analysis of external phenomena, even though both can be discussed logically and discursively.

What is more, the implications of contemplative science are far-reaching, even ultimate. We begin with the question of truth. Contemplative science points us toward the realization of truth for ourselves. If there is truth, then it is truth not for a particular individual alone, but for everyone, even if individuals describe or emphasize different aspects of it. This is a key point; it is what makes perennial philosophy perennial. And if some have realized truth, then they represent cultural elders, so to speak, a natural élite. Further, any educational system would need to be reoriented toward the realization of truth and its implications.

If we take seriously the implications of contemplative science as outlined here, it becomes radical, revolutionary. The way we see all aspects of society—beginning with education, politics, economics, religion—are transformed, even overturned. For instance, imagine what academic institutions would look like if they were oriented toward the inner life and toward the ultimate realization of truth. Imagine what political life would look like if politics were an expression of a culture devoted primarily toward the realization and expression of truth, oriented toward truth. What would be the economics of a society oriented toward the recognition and expression of truth? Of course, this leads us inevitably toward the question of what that truth is.

In his essay "The Poet," Ralph Waldo Emerson remarked that we tend to regard the material world as "self-existent," and as a result we think sensually; our sciences do not recognize that the earth and the heavenly bodies are but the "retinues" of the higher Being to which we have access. We habitually do not think in terms that allow transcendence. But in fact, he continues, the apparent conflict between materialistic science and religion can be resolved by a higher science, a science that "goes abreast with the just elevation of the man, keeping step with religion and metaphysics." In other words, science need not be superficial; it can be "an index of our self-knowledge." This self-knowledge is also knowledge of the transcendent.

On what is this higher science based? It is based in the contemplative ascent, in our capacity to enter into the "symmetry and truth" that is in and above nature. Emerson points us toward "a very high sort of seeing, which does not come by study, but by the intellect being where and what it sees, by sharing the path or circuit of things through forms, and so making them translucid to others." Emerson is referring here to the Platonic understanding that above the material world is the realm of transcendent ideas, the enduring presence of which is reflected in the world that we see. The Orphic poet participates in creation itself by opening up to the transcendent realm out of which the material world ceaselessly comes into being. And a higher science has to acknowledge this same kind of higher seeing, the contemplative vision.

This higher seeing is in fact more than seeing; it is to open oneself up to what is beyond one's own consciousness, to go beyond one's own "privacy of power" to a "great public power" on which one can draw, by allowing the "ethereal tides" to roll and circulate through us, so that we are caught up into the life of the universe, where our "speech is thunder," our "thoughts are laws," and our words as "universally intelligible as the plants and animals." The philosopher-poet, the true intellectual, is so by opening up to the divine mind, by perceiving with, as Emerson puts it in quotations, "the flower of the mind," referring of course to that famous phrase in *The Chaldean Oracles,* the oracular text beloved of the Platonists. Perceiving with the flower of the mind is just what Damascius also counseled, we will recall. He who perceives in this way is not only human, but, as Emerson puts it, is in fact one of the "liberating gods."

Such a one, understood either as a philosopher or as a poet, is like the Druid who is "free throughout the world." But what is the nature of this freedom? It is an unfettering of consciousness and an opening into the "transcendental and extraordinary." In fact, Emerson writes, only this freedom is of value in what we read or write, this being carried away and inflamed by the liberation of thought; it is the secret not only of philosophy and poetry but of religion itself. The freedom of which Emerson writes is the emancipation of consciousness from separation into transcendent unity. And how does one achieve this?

In *The Cloud of Unknowing,* we read that there is no means to obtaining contemplative knowledge; it comes through grace alone. It comes by us giving up our "own being," that is, our selfishness or self-centeredness. The text warns us not to follow bodily interpretations of what is "ghostly," that is, spiritual (*geistlich*). It warns against misunderstanding "inward," a concept that could mislead one to strive "against nature," just as "up" might lead one to think of things "in a bodily manner" as "upward," when in fact there is no direction in this spiritual work. In this work the soul is "oned to God," because they are not two. The "ghostly [spiritual] work" is "nowhere bodily;" its place cannot be discovered. The *Cloud* was not written for "fleshly janglers, flatterers and blamers, ronkers and ronners," but only for those who are inclined by nature toward contemplative work.

This contemplative practice is described in detail, not in *The Cloud of Unknowing* itself, but in a companion work, *The Book of Privy Counsel,* which although it is certainly is couched in Christian language, clearly reflects the Dionysian tradition that is, Platonism adapted to a Christian context. It tells us that "contemplative prayer is the naked and blind intuitive perception of God's being as our own being and our own source, without words." We are to simply and purely perceive our own naked being prior to words or concepts, without any fragmentation or division of mind. This is a perception not of what we are, but *that* we are, elementally. We are to remain whole and recollected in the depths of our being, continuously centered, through both activity and contemplation, in the awareness of our naked pure being identical with the divine. Through this we attain the highest perfection of union with God in consummate love, which cannot be conveyed in language, only alluded to. Ultimately, it is beyond our awareness of our own being, beyond any mental constructs whatever.

This transcendence is truth. It is truth, distinguished not by what it is, but by what it is not. That is the essence of the *via negativa*, or way of negation, at the center of perennial philosophy. It is at the center of the works of the great medieval mystics Meister Eckhart, John Tauler, and the author of *The Cloud* and *The Book of Privy Counsel;* and at the heart of the works of more recent mystics like Jacob Böhme, who referred to transcendence as the *nichts* (nothing), and as the *ungrund,* or not-ground. It is visible too in the work of Ralph Waldo Emerson, whose very first book testified to his own experience of self-transcendence.

Of course, truth—even referring to truth—is out of fashion these days. So perhaps we will have to whisper. Commonly, many intellectuals claim that truth is relative, that each individual has a truth of his own, that it is not possible to arrive at the truth, and even if it were, that in turn would generate an élite, which is by egalitarian definition, bad. All that and more said, however, since it is possible to conceive of truth, then it is at least possible that truth exists. Truth, in this context, is knowable by what it is not, that is, by negation. Truth is not an object, not a subject, not perceived through the senses, not a mental construct of any kind. But this means that we need to revise how we understand what truth is, and in this way we can begin to approach it. This dropping of misconceptions about truth is another way of describing contemplative science.

Ultimately, contemplative science, though it can be described as inner attention, requires giving up preconceptions and notions about who we are in relation to the world. It is not about adding new concepts, but about dropping misconceptions. Hence it is not easily susceptible to discursive analysis driven by ratiocination alone; ratiocination is fundamentally dualistic, based on the relationship of self and other, or subject and object. "I" calculate "my" relationship to "it," the other. But contemplative science, though it incorporates discursive analysis and ratiocination up to a point, is nonetheless is beyond them.

Hence science as usually understood cannot reach contemplative experience because it is about changes in consciousness that are beyond what can be measured or quantified, even if traces may be left behind, much like underwater movement. This is certainly true of contemplative experience along the lines described earlier, both with regard to the contemplative ascent and with regard to transcendence. As soon as one begins to go beyond subject/object divisions, which is what both of those terms mean, then one is in a region of consciousness that can be pointed toward by discursive reason but that cannot be captured by it.

But contemplative experience is verifiable, and in this sense the term "contemplative science" is appropriate—it is a science in the etymological sense of *scientia,* whose root is *scire,* to know. It is a science in the sense that many authors verified the contemplative tradition over the course of generations and millennia. And it is a science even in the restrictive contemporary sense of a body of methodical observations and propositions concerning a specific subject. To develop such empirical observations and propositions about inner experience is no less valid than to develop them about external objects or phenomena.

For all his indignant provocations, Friedrich Nietzsche had intuited something of inner life and what it means. Highly critical of monotheism, especially Judaism and Christianity, he held that especially for their adherents, faith and truth represent very different paths. If faith is exalted, he wrote, then reason and knowledge are discredited, and truth becomes a forbidden road. The Brahmins knew this, Plato knew this, "every student of the esoteric knows it," Nietzsche asserted. In *Beyond Good and Evil,* Nietzsche distinguished between the exoteric and the esoteric, the former consisting in seeing things from below upward, the latter in seeing *from above* downward.

What Nietzsche alludes to is indeed an awkward truth about contemplative science: it is hierarchical. There is an above and a below, there are sages and fools, and those in between. The purpose of contemplative science is not just knowledge for its own sake, but the attaining of wisdom through contemplative ascent. Contemplative science centers on existential transformation and illumination, which is the path to wisdom. And furthermore, the view from a lower vantage point might well be quite different from that of a higher one. Hence contemplative science is fundamentally different than scientific investigation focused on knowledge of external phenomena, including neuroscience, for contemplative science entails changes in individual consciousness; it requires individual transformation.

Contemplative science, like externally focused science, conducts experiments, seeks verifiable processes and principles, and develops a systematic understanding based on those experiments, processes, and principles. Verifiability is as important to contemplative science as it is to externally focused science. Both are empirical. But whereas externally focused science centers on objects, contemplative science centers on the perception and consciousness of the subject with an eye to answering ultimate questions of meaning, which are traditionally held to be answerable not through the study of objects or physical laws, but through contemplative illumination.

Understood in this sense, perennial philosophy rightfully can be seen as the head of the sciences not least because contemplative science is simultaneously self-knowledge and knowledge of what transcends the self. The Delphic injunction to know thyself, γνῶθι σεαυτόν, is paradoxical because ultimately what one comes to know is beyond what we can term "self." This is clear from the *via negativa* contemplative tradition as represented not only in Platonism, but also in the works of Dionysius the Areopagite, Meister Eckhart, and the anonymous author of *The Cloud of Unknowing*. Perennial philosophy is the head of the sciences because it concerns the ultimate mysteries: who we really are, and how we can understand and realize truth, beauty, goodness—and wisdom, the crown of them all.

Contemplative science is a way of describing human purpose and meaning without a specific religious context; but it nonetheless is historically embedded in different religious contexts, be they Greek, Western European, British, or American. But by concentrating on the most fundamental elements of perennial philosophy, we can see how it could be applied in other religious contexts as well. Obviously, perennial philosophy has its roots in the past, but our approach allows us to turn now to what it has to offer for the future. As we will see, it has more to offer than we might have thought.

# Chapter Seven

# Perennial Philosophy in the Future

Although it has political, economic, and cultural implications, perennial philosophy is not itself political, economic, or even cultural. It is, rather, contact with what is prior to politics, economics, or culture. Perennial philosophy at its heart is contact with what is prior to anything we today would call "philosophy" or "religion," for that matter. Perennial philosophy (if we want to continue using that term) is about how to approach and realize truth itself. Ultimately, this is and will always be an individual journey. This individual journey existed in the past, and sometimes generated cultural renaissances; it exists today; and it will exist in the future. The individual search for and realization of truth will continue as long as human beings do, and that is the key to perennial philosophy in the future.

It became conventional, particularly in progressive or leftist intellectual circles late in the twentieth century to inveigh against "essentialism," which often was derided as "the essentialist fallacy." The underlying premise of "anti-essentialism" was egalitarianism—but beyond the notion that everyone is or must be made "equal" was often a somewhat concealed nihilism. Nihilism here means that if one rejects the concept of metaphysical truth, and if one consequently also rejects the concept of metaphysical ideas or essences, then one is left more or less adrift. Behind anti-essentialism, in other words, is a tacit nihilism, sometimes expressed in more or less extreme forms of relativism, in other cases expressed outright as flamboyant antinomianism.

If "essentialism" is defined in reductive materialistic terms loosely derived from Aristotle, then it is held to be that things or individuals have inherent properties arising from particular sets of conditions—but such a definition actually is a way of avoiding the real question by reduction to the merely physical and to discursive analysis. The real question of "essentialism" is metaphysical. Anti-essentialism is typically justified by a kind of constructionist argument—that human beings construct their own truths and their own realities. And of course there is some validity to this notion, since in fact we *do* interpret what we see; we *do* seek to see patterns and to make sense of what we perceive.

But does that mean therefore there is no metaphysical truth? To make such a claim derives from an implicit belief that all human cognition is discursive reason colored by passions like anger, fear, jealousy, greed, and so forth—that "I construct my own reality." But what if there's more possible for human cognition? What if contemplative ascent is possible, and what if the contemplative journey is prepared for and accompanied by the realization of what are often termed "virtues," meaning kindness, love, compassion, expressed as generosity? And if contemplative ascent is possible, prepared for and accompanied by a cultivation of virtue, perhaps then too the realization of truth is *also* possible.

And here we begin to discover that perennial philosophy, once we begin to understand it on its own terms, dramatically transforms how we see everything. It is as if our vision, once blurry, suddenly becomes clear—and what we before didn't recognize as nonsense, when we see things in this new way, reveals itself to be just that. Even if some, or most, or even every single other person asserts that there is no such thing as metaphysical truth, and no way to realize it, that doesn't change the possibility that nonetheless there actually may be truth.

What does "truth" mean here? It does not mean *a* truth, but rather an ultimate reality. The collective testimony of the Platonic tradition, as we have seen, is that there is ultimate reality, it is beyond the grasp of discursive reason, it cannot be conveyed adequately in language, it is beyond subject and object, and it can be alluded to, in code words, like transcendence. The Platonic tradition holds that it is possible to ascend through contemplation, that one can see inwardly realms that are more enduring than what we see in this mutable and fleeting world, and that ultimately it is possible to glimpse and perhaps even to realize the nature of ultimate reality, which we can allude to as transcendence.

This possibility—of contemplative ascent to and potential realization of truth—has quite a few implications for society as a whole. We already saw, in "Above and Below," that in the Platonic tradition earthly life reflects its celestial archetypes, and that from Pythagoras to Plato to Plotinus, we find the recurrent idea of cultural renaissance centered in the possibility of realizing a community with contemplative ascent and transcendence at its center. But we did not then explore, as we now will, how such a spiritually centered culture would shape the ways we understand art, literature, economics, and politics.

In so many domains of life today, it is as if every means of directional orientation has been lost, so that one is left to one's own impulses alone. The lure of contemporary artistic expression is that it becomes self-expression alone, and even a kind of narcissism. In the contemporary world, there would seem to be no such thing as a canon, the word "canon" meaning a standard of measurement, from the Greek *kanon,* κανών. Indeed, in the arts, in painting, in sculpture, across the spectrum there is no accepted canon or even a way of establishing one, just as in literature, and those who defend the very idea of a canon are regarded as impossibly backward. The future, it would seem, is ever more individualist iconoclasm, more provocation, even to the point of degradation, so that what once was shocking or totally chaotic becomes humdrum, meaning that "I" must make a name for myself with something even more outrageous. And there is no way to gauge meaning or value. These may seem exaggerations, but are they?

With regard to art, perennial philosophy has much to say. But to understand it, one must look back over what we have suggested already about perennial philosophy and its expression in Pythagoreanism and in ancient European cultures. According to Pythagorean tradition, and indeed according to both ancient Greek and for that matter classical Buddhist sculpture as well, the cosmos reflects archetypal mathematical ratios and principles. Earthly beauty is beautiful, in these traditions, when it best, most clearly manifests celestial or transcendent, that is, timeless beauty. When we see a classical Greek or Buddhist statue, its perfect features and proportions are so because they reflect a geometrical-mathematical canon. When that proportionality is not heeded, the result is awry. What is depicted is also invoked; it guides us toward a cultural and spiritual aspiration to be like what we see, to realize it for ourselves.

There is a new way to understand the arts by way of perennial philosophy, in which the arts reflect and support the contemplative ascent toward transcendence. What makes a work of art truly great, from this perspective, is the degree to which in contemplating it, we are united with what it manifests, the degree to which, in it, in experiencing it, the apparent divide between subject and object is forgotten or begins to vanish. The measure of a work of art is how much we become lost in it—and what is lost is our selfishness, our ordinary "I" ruled by the passions and the demands of the moment. Instead, we are lifted up, out of ourselves, toward the celestial or transcendent, into the realm of the gods.

This does not necessarily mean that a great work of art is static; it can be more static or more dynamic; it may embody the dark as well as the light; it may be frightening or even terrifying; it may be tragic, or comedic; it even may be horrific. But it nonetheless acts, seen in a larger cultural context, to transport us beyond ourselves. And in this transport, however it comes about, we come closer to the transcendence of self and other; we feel by experiencing the art, we have come closer to the gods. And of course the gods themselves are not static but dynamic, sometimes experienced as serene beauty and timelessness to be sure, but sometimes also experienced as the shattering of our conventional self in ways that may be disconcerting, alarming, even terrifying. The poet Rainer Maria Rilke conveyed this beautifully about encountering an angel, angels having much the role of the Platonic gods.

What I am suggesting, in other words, is that the natural canon of the arts is based on the contemplative ascent in which self and other, subject and object, knower and known, increasingly reveal themselves to be one. The highest art is that which most closely or completely unites us with the divine beauty, goodness, and truth that shines through it. Great art exalts us, not because we are ourselves great, but because our identities become more transparent and what is beyond us comes through more clearly. The measure of great art is exaltation; the measure of great art is the degree of expansion into what transcends us as individuals.

The nature of the art itself, of course, varies from culture to culture. We are ennobled by classical Greek statuary and high-pillared temples; we are ennobled, too, by a Buddhist stupa's intricate and beautiful geometrical symbolism; we are ennobled by the serene, slightly smiling countenance of a gilded Buddha-statue on an altar; and we are ennobled by the magnificent vast landscape paintings of the Hudson River School, the artistic complement to American Transcendentalism. By "canon," I do not mean a rigid prescription for art; rather, I mean the measure of great art on the scale of exaltation, on the scale of transcendence of self and other.

Some art is discordant; and some is harmonious. Dionysius the Areopagite pointed this out when he observed in *Celestial Hierarchy* that some symbols of the divine are beautiful, but others are discordant, even shocking, because they convey in another way aspects of the divine that call for them. But both are part of the *via positiva,* the affirmative way through images toward transcendent union. We seem to have forgotten that art can serve as a contemplative support, and by engaging in it, by experiencing it, it can resonate and awaken in us a kind of contemplative ascent. Art is not itself contemplation, but it is very much akin to it.

So it is also with the written arts. Poetry, fiction, novels, these too have a canon. But the canon is not as the term is usually employed. The literary canon as it is ordinarily taught in higher education typically refers loosely to those works considered "classics," but "classics" in such a context generally means that others have taught them in the past, and so now we should do so, without really considering in what sense a work is *really* classic—from the Latin *classicus,* a word referring to the ideal in its class.

What makes a poem or a work of fiction ideal in its class, or to use another term, archetypal? There is by now so much confusion and disarray in contemporary notions of a literary canon that literature has nearly dissolved as a field; the very idea of a literary canon is in disrepute. Because there is no consensus as to what belongs in a literary canon, or indeed whether the very idea of a canon makes any sense, the study of literature has been fragmented. There are, it would seem, few shared standards or even ways of arriving at standards. But there is an entirely different way of understanding what a literary canon means, with the assistance of perennial philosophy.

To consider literature anew, we must look back to its origins in the West, which are also the origins of Platonism—in Orphism. The golden chain of philosopher-poet-seers began with Orpheus, and included also Pythagoras, Plato, and Plotinus. Now it is time to look back to the mysterious figure of Orpheus, whom we introduced in "Transcendence." Orpheus was a poet and musician, whose songs were accompanied by his lyre, the strings of which produce cosmic harmonies, calling and soothing beasts and birds. He was the mythic origin of the Orphic mysteries, the initiatory tradition at the center of which was the transcendence of self.

Initiates into the Mysteries were often described as divinely intoxicated, *en theos,* from which we derive the English word "enthusiastic." In its purest meaning, enthusiastic means filled with the divine, and Orpheus's poetry and music, as well as celebrating the Orphic Mysteries, was a form of epiclesis (ἐπίκλησις), invoking the god(s). Poetry in this context is magical, invocatory and evocatory; it is "words of power," the *mythos* and *logos* together. Its power and purity can be gauged by the extent to which it divinely intoxicates us, pulls us upward into the divine, calls the divine down into us, awakens transcendent spaciousness in us.

Approaching literature with these root concepts in mind transforms how we think of it. At once the way we see poetry is akin to how we earlier began to see works of art, and also how we can see music—the more powerful it is, the more evocative, the more it carries us beyond our ordinary sense of self. What it awakens in us is intimately inward, and at once transcendent, spacious, full of light. Great poetry, like great music, moves us into an ecstasy that can also be described as an enstasy, at once inwardness and beyondness, intimate and yet impersonal, in us and yet far beyond us, in short, into the divine.

Such a movement beyond self is an exaltation, not of us, but of our experience. Such a movement could include implacability, terror, wrath, joy, serenity, indifference, love, and yet is ultimately beyond any of these. Great poetry, great literature, pulls us beyond our conventional world, opens up into a spaciousness that can't be captured fully in words, only evoked. We experience such Orphic moments in the works of Emerson and Thoreau, especially in *Walden,* when the "whole body is as one sense, and imbibes delight through every pore;" we experience them with Rilke, and with Yeats; there are moments with Eliot, and with Kathleen Raine. We experience this exaltation also with Shakespeare, and Melville, in *Moby Dick,* and McCarthy, for instance in *Blood Meridian;* it can be dark. Great literature is initiatory; in it, we experience exaltation, an expansion of what it can mean to be human, and glimpses of what is more than human.

How are such experiences through art, literature, and music "measured"? After all, a canon implies measurements, standards. Traditionally, the answer is *paradosis* (παράδοσις), that is, tradition itself, what is passed on as most valuable, that most speaks to us of different kinds of exaltation, that most awakens a sense of luminosity and spaciousness in us. That is what the Platonic Academy meant, too—it was not so much an institution as a way of conveying the tradition to the next generation. Paradosis is at heart informal, organic; and if we understand the core principle of what is being transmitted, then it is quite clear where it is being transmitted, too. This was sometimes also called the "golden chain of philosophers," which sometimes included figures like Hermes Trismegistus because its purpose is to indicate modes of transcendence, not individual human beings. The "chain" is horizontal (temporal), but every figure in it represents a vertical opening into timelessness. What is valuable in the chain is measured individually by the degree to which it evokes timelessness in us, and cumulatively, by the treasuring of generations gone before.

Such ideas concerning art, literature, and music would seem rather remote from economics as understood in the contemporary world, and of course that is the case. Indeed, one frequently hears that the purpose of higher education has nothing to do with the liberal arts, or the humanities, but rather is to be measured on the basis of whether one is fitted for a particular job, whether one learns particular useful skills measured, in the end, by the utilitarian standard of whether one is hired. And of course this is one kind of measurement for higher education, even if were it strictly followed, there would be no difference between higher education and trade school.

But in fact such ideas about art, literature, and music have economic implications as well. One could argue that there is an economics of perennial philosophy, and here too, what we are considering is transformative. For the most part, contemporary economics may be understood as the study of the exchange and consumption of objects. Contemporary economics is the objectification of everything—other people, forests, soil, animals, water, anything that can be commodified, packaged, exploited, manipulated, and consumed. And of course art, literature, and music all can be objectified as well. That is the nature of the consumerist system.

Perennial philosophy isn't directly opposed to consumerism. Rather, it reminds us that there is also another way to understand art, literature, music, indeed, human life itself. It doesn't matter so much if art, literature, or music are commodified if they nonetheless can serve as supports for our contemplative ascent, if through experiencing them, we experience exaltation; if through them, we are ennobled. It reminds us that the purpose of human life, ultimately, is contemplative ascent and awakening to transcendence, and so it is not opposed but indifferent to consumerism.

A culture animated by perennial philosophy is naturally oriented toward spiritual realization. Its economy is shaped not by desire, greed, and envy for objects of exchange so much as oriented toward recognizing and supporting contemplative realization. This is not to say that such a culture, or any human culture, is perfect, but that nonetheless there are examples of such cultures, noble experiments in human history we might term them. Historical Buddhism in Tibet is one such example; another is Bhutanese Buddhism, a noble experiment to this day. These are cultures oriented toward contemplative practice and realization; their rich and complex cultures no doubt were and are not perfect, but they nonetheless exemplify human possibility in this regard.

What characterizes the economics of a culture animated by perennial philosophy? To think about this, we should consider what is valued most in such a culture. Such a culture is not driven by the passions, for instance, by the greed or envy that much advertising capitalizes on, so much as by the passion for transcendence expressed through active forms of the arts (martial or otherwise) as well as through practices including meditation in stillness. Such a culture has an aspirational center, which is wisdom that flows from transcendence. The economy of such a culture would need to be understood in the larger context of such values and aspirations.

A central mark of such a culture can be expressed as kindness or compassion extended not only to one's own family or kin, nor even only to one's larger tribe or community, but also to all other people, and indeed, beyond humanity to the earth, trees, waters, winds, fish, birds, animals, outward in every direction. The basis of such widely extended benevolence is actually metaphysical, because it originates in the transcendence of subject and object that is at the center of perennial philosophy. A "mark" of mature self-other transcendence, in Buddhism, is that the insight is inseparable from compassion. In Platonism, something similar is expressed in the allegory of the Cave, when the individual who has been outside the Cave goes back inside to convey the experience to the others and point them toward freedom.

The point here is that perennial philosophy is not separate from values that support the cultivation of virtue, but in fact is all of a piece in this regard. Near the end of his book on perennial philosophy, Aldous Huxley remarked that in such a tradition, "it is axiomatic that the end of human life is contemplation, or the direct and intuitive awareness of God; that action is the means to that end; that a society is good to the extent that it renders contemplation possible for its members; and that the existence of at least a minority of contemplatives is necessary for the well-being of any society." Such a perspective may be 180° from "the popular philosophy of our own time," but then, too, the economics it encourages is also 180° from that of the popular economics of our time.

Our popular economic model (in nations putatively

capitalist and communist alike) disaggregates everything, so that it can be commodified, that is, rendered an object for sale. That is as true of putatively communist as of capitalist societies; it is evident not only in the broader privileging of action over contemplation, and of exploitation and consumption over reverence for nature and for what we inherit from our own ancestors; but also can be measured in the degree to which a society is willing to disaggregate a particular "resource" from its larger context. Such a disaggregation is visible in the strip mining of an Appalachian mountain and the obliteration of a whole natural and human area in order to extract coal; and it is visible in an even more extreme way in those who would kill other human beings (as in Russia, China, and Cambodia) to further some fanatical mirage of a future utopia. In all such cases, there is little or no kindness, no appreciation for others.

But the same is not true of those cultures at the center of which is some variant of perennial philosophy. Here the term "culture" need not be understood too grandly; one sees such local cultures in all communities in which people's artisanship, their love for the local landscape and waters, their spiritual practices, all reflect the higher values of a contemplative life. That a group, a community, a region, even a small nation can reflect such values is evident wherever such groups or communities spontaneously develop, be it in a city in Morocco, in rural England, in upstate New York or in the mountains of California, whether in Switzerland or in Bhutan. Such groups, communities, and even small nations can embody care for the natural world as well as care for other people, and encourage those who feel a call to a contemplative life.

Because perennial philosophy guides people toward a contemplative life, it encourages in a culture what conduces to contemplation not only in the ways one might immediately think of, but also as expressed in ordinary life as contemplative artisanship. To shape wood or metal, to farm, all the walks of life one can imagine also can serve as contemplative practices in themselves because to engage in them is to immerse oneself in them as concentrated attention and flow. Here, what matters is not a "job" in the modern sense, nor is it abstract monetary rewards, though those may come, but absorption into and mastery of work as a support for contemplative life.

In turn, when we turn from economics to politics, we can see that in the light of perennial philosophy, politics and governance look quite different than those to which we are accustomed in a consumerist political system where the most unscrupulous and shallow of confidence men often claw their way to the top. By contrast, a politics based in perennial philosophy looks for guidance to those most deeply engaged in the contemplative life. For them, such a role might well seem a burden, certainly it's a responsibility, and it isn't necessarily a role they seek. The aspiration is governance based in wisdom, and one can see something along those lines in the Bhutanese model of a guiding royal family. But there is also a collective wisdom in the people, and we see that reflected in the Swiss system of allowing public referenda and votes on major issues confronting the country and people. Both of these examples are in accord with perennial philosophy, which, from Pythagoras and Plato on, supported the political system that best would enable governance based in wisdom. In some cases, that might be a benevolent king or queen; in others, it might be a group of elders; in still others, it might be a rule by consensus like that of the Swiss referenda. Every political system can turn despotic, including rule by the masses. What is necessary, perennial philosophy tells us, is the inherent cultural value system directed toward and by contemplative aspiration, ideally for all, but at least for some. If a culture's values are awry, its political system is virtually certain to become despotic.

One lesson from the contemporary era is that political gigantism is not sustainable. We saw this with the fall of the Soviet Union's empire; we saw this also with the decline of the British empire; and we see this with the decline of the American empire too. Once a political system becomes too gigantic, too disconnected from the people and from the sources that sustain it, it is captured by individuals and groups that milk it for their own ends. Policy decisions are based not on the long-term good of the people and of nature, but on what is politically expedient or worse, on what one group can obtain for itself at the expense of the others.

By contrast, perennial philosophy encourages political decentralization. We will recall that Plato imagined not the ideal empire, but the ideal city, and that Plotinus sought to found Platonopolis. A city or a locality is best suited for wise governance because there is local responsibility and accountability. By and large, a city or a township is far less likely than an unaccountable, gigantic, and remote bureaucracy to engage in unsustainable behavior, like rewarding those who don't work more than those who do, or seeking to establish an imperial presence around the world. Perennial philosophy humbly suggests that smaller is better.

*
* *

Perennial philosophy is not ideological or doctrinaire; it has no millenarian agenda. It is not grounded in dreams of material consumption as progress. Rather, it represents an entirely different way of understanding human purpose in the world. It is applicable to the arts, to literature, and more broadly to cultural, economic, and political life because it allows us to evaluate the meaning of what we do in light of contemplative ascent and realization. Yet at the same time, it is not wedded to any particular religious construct, any more than it is bound to any particular artistic, literary, cultural, economic, or political type.

That independence is what makes it perennial; it is also what makes the alternative term "contemplative science" appropriate too. One could envision new cultures emerging from contemplative science expressed in a Buddhist, a Hindu, a Christian, a European Pagan, or for that matter, a non-aligned ambience unidentifiable with any particular preëxisting religious tradition. If perennial philosophy is indeed perennial, if it is represented, broadly speaking, by contemplative ascent and realization as we have seen, then it can develop anew in a variety of cultural matrices. That, in fact, is why we find it recurring across time and space.

Too often, perennial philosophy is described as if it were a syncretic amalgam of different traditions, or again, as if it represents the residue or trace of a universal tradition in the hoary past. But as we have seen, the perennial philosophy is more productively seen as fundamentally experiential, as representing an individual map for understanding contemplative practice and its significances. Seen in this light, its broader cultural implications, however important they might be, are ultimately only secondary. When we talk about a perennial philosophy, we are really referring to "philosophy" as once the term was understood, as a way of life centered in love (*philo-*) for wisdom (*sophia*).

None of this may resonate with you; indeed, you might be inclined to dismiss it all out of hand. Still, perhaps in reading this you have felt something stir in you; perhaps it is oddly familiar to you; and perhaps you feel the inclination to investigate further. You might turn to the dialogues of that sly old rascal Plato, to the austere beauty of Plotinus's *Enneads,* to the dense prose of Damascius, to the pure descriptions of Dionysius the Areopagite, to the gnomic words of Meister Eckhart, or to the sage advice of the author of *The Book of Privy Counsel.* You could do worse. But beware: once you begin, you might find whole new worlds and ways of seeing this world open up for you. It might begin the most extraordinary journey one could undertake. Who knows? At the very least, one might find oneself poking one's head, even for a moment, out of the Cave.

# Chapter Eight

# Conclusion

To this point, our purpose has been to introduce perennial philosophy as metaphysics and cosmology, as spiritual path toward realization, and as a cultural source and inspiration. I have presented perennial philosophy in its most essential aspect, as contemplative, experiential path, and indicated some of its implications. And I have offered that introduction in as clear and straightforward way possible. But now, near the conclusion of our journey, we will think about how perennial philosophy might be studied and understood going forward, how it can be understood in this strange, confusing new world in which we find ourselves today.

The truth is, what we have considered in this book has not been studied extensively in the academy, let alone taught consistently, over the past few centuries. Occasionally authors have been accepted into the literary or philosophical canon who smuggle in perennial philosophy under covers, so to speak. One thinks here of Emerson, for instance, whose work is suffused by Platonism. But Emerson is relatively little taught, these days, and occasionally one even runs across ill-considered diatribes by putative English professors against teaching his work at all. Plato might creep in the back door, but it is rare for Plotinus, Damascius, or Dionysius the

Areopagite to rate even a mention, let alone a place in the curriculum. Maybe that is part of the power of perennial philosophy—perhaps it is always a little renegade, a bit of an outlaw.

Furthermore, it is surprising how little scholarship on mysticism there has been in the last century. Here, I am using the word "mysticism" as synonymous with perennial philosophy as we have discussed it in this book, that is, with the contemplative ascent and with transcendence. Understood in this way, mysticism has a fairly precise meaning, still abstract to be sure, but nonetheless, not to be understood as emotional furor but as the contemplative ascent above emotional attachment and aversion, into the imaginal realm, and beyond that, into the sphere of negative theology.

There are, of course, some authors whose work focuses on what we may term Platonic mysticism. One is Willigis Jäger, who is a former Roman Catholic contemplative and lineage holder in Japanese Zen Buddhism who developed a contemplative tradition that may best be described as perennial philosophy in practice. He makes clear in his books that he is entirely familiar with the tradition of Platonic mysticism. And another such author is B. Alan Wallace, a teacher in the Tibetan Buddhist tradition who also has published extensively on contemplative practices in a contemporary, non-sectarian context. Like Jäger, Wallace has deep knowledge and experience in a Buddhist contemplative tradition, but also refers back to the Western tradition of Platonic mysticism. The advent of Asian religions, and particularly Buddhist meditative traditions in the West illuminates the contemplative traditions of the West, in particular, Platonic mysticism.

And since it is the case that there is a broad Platonic tradition we can trace from Plato and Plotinus through Damascius, and then from Dionysius the Areopagite forward through via negative Christian mysticism, up to and past Emerson into the present day, it should not be ignored. This is not to say that the Platonic tradition is identical to Buddhism—only Buddhism developed concepts like interdependent origination, or the non-existence of the self as a permanent entity, or emptiness. Platonism, which for our purposes is roughly identical with perennial philosophy, is its own tradition, but has some overlap with Buddhism and with Vedanta as well.

There is an ultimate question that perennial philosophy raises, and that is almost never acknowledged: do all human beings have access to truth or not? If the answer is no, then it follows that each contemplative approach goes in a different direction, toward a different truth. But multiple truths then become "truths," and so bracketed, one ends in nihilism. On the other hand, if the answer is yes, that all have access to truth, then one has to ask whether truth differs, or whether it is one. If it is one, and all potentially have access to it through introspective contemplation, then what perennial philosophy points toward is the human capacity for realizing this truth, the underlying ground of existence.

Of course, perennial philosophy has as its center what I have been terming the contemplative ascent, which implies degrees or gradations. Hence it is possible that what we see suggested in Platonism (because there is no clear prescription in Platonism for contemplative practice itself) is more fragmented or momentary than what we see in the far vaster, more developed and refined contemplative tradition of Buddhism, but nonetheless is akin to it. Buddhism, after all, has the rich history of countless meditative practitioners who in turn left rich literary records of contemplative practice and realization. Still, I am not arguing that Platonism and Buddhism are identical.

Rather, I am raising the essential question of perennial philosophy: is there truth, and if so, is there a path to realizing it? If what is true is true for us all as human beings; and if we all at least potentially have access to it; and if further we all can follow a path to realizing it, then in this sense perennial philosophy is nothing other than the highest assertion of human potential. And in this light, perennial philosophy can be understood as empirical in an ultimate sense: its sine qua non is contemplative ascent and transcendent experience.

As we've seen, neither perennial philosophy nor the contemplative ascent and realization at its center are opposed to science or to reason, as they are sometimes presented to be. In fact, it would be much more accurate to see perennial philosophy as corresponding to science in that it affirms the empirical verification of its theses, the continuous refining of its premises based on direct contemplative experience. This is what we see also in Buddhism, of course, made more visible by the collaborative explorations of neuroscientists and Buddhist practitioners beginning in the late twentieth century. H.H. the Fourteenth Dalai Lama famously said that "If scientific analysis were conclusively to demonstrate certain claims in Buddhism to be false, then we must accept the findings of science and abandon those claims." And the Dalai Lama forecast an emerging "science of consciousness" that does not require religion as such. Perennial philosophy, needless to say, points in the same direction.

The term "perennial philosophy" is not perhaps ideal, but it has its virtues. It evokes the enduring nature of the subject, and it separates the topic from religious fideism at least to some extent, while at the same time recalling the original meaning of philosophy as "love of wisdom." As such, perennial philosophy may belong more to the future than to the past, precisely because it is consonant with a scientific approach and well suited to the empirical investigation of consciousness. Perennial philosophy is as much a set of guidelines as it is a model for beginning to understand consciousness in more profound ways.

But it may be that in the end, the term "perennial philosophy," like "mysticism," will have to be left behind because it accreted too many misleading associations. What I have done, in this book, is seek to pare back those accretions and reveal in clear language the essential contemplative path and result that is visible throughout the Platonic tradition. Still, I am not that attached to the terms here. If "perennial philosophy" and "mysticism" are, in the end, still too laden by confusing accretions, then perhaps it is better to use a term like "contemplative science." In any case, there can be no doubt that what we have described in this little book is present in the works of Plato, Plotinus, and Damascius; it is present in the works of Meister Eckhart; it is recognizable in the works of Emerson; it is still present to us today; and it no doubt will be present to you in the distant future, when the many nihilistic fashions of the moment are long since forgotten. Perennial philosophy is, after all, perennially renewed. But then, you've always known all of this, haven't you?

22789341R00076

Printed in Great Britain
by Amazon